For Ann

The Sportsman's Ideal

Ian Dussek

Motor Racing Publications

MOTOR RACING PUBLICATIONS LTD
Unit 6, The Pilton Estate, 46 Pitlake, Croydon CR0 3RY, England

This work is published with the assistance of the Michael Sedgwick Memorial Trust.

Founded in memory of the famous motoring researcher and author Michael Sedgwick (1926-1983), the Trust is a registered charity to encourage new research and recording of motoring history.

Suggestions for future projects, and donations, should be sent to the Honorary Secretary of the Michael Sedgwick Memorial Trust, c/o the John Montagu Building, Beaulieu, Hampshire SO4 7ZN, England.

ISBN 0 947981 04 7
First published 1985

Editor: John Plummer

Photosetting by Zee Creative Ltd, London SW16
Printed in Great Britain by Netherwood, Dalton & Co Ltd, Bradley Mills, Huddersfield, West Yorkshire

Contents

Foreword

by Michael E. Ware
Curator, National Motor Museum

I was very surprised and felt very honoured to be asked to contribute a foreword for this book. Surprised because no-one has ever asked me to contribute a foreword to anything before and honoured because this is the first book which has benefited from funding from the Michael Sedgwick Memorial Trust.

The H.R.G. has always been a favourite of mine, ever since I first saw one climbing Fingle Hill on an Exeter Trial soon after the war, my first-ever encounter with motor sport. I was very sorry to see the last of the traditional models produced in 1956 though delighted that the firm went on for 10 years in general engineering, also keeping up a comprehensive spares service for owners. Unlike most other specialist sports car firms, it went out solvent and basically in the same ownership, never having been the subject of take-overs or major boardroom reshuffles to produce more finance. They were a firm who loved to see their versatile cars involved in all aspects of motor sport and whilst they never ran a works team, they would support private entrants and even provided some back-up on Alpine rallies in the form of a service van — possibly the first works to do so.

The survival of something like five-sixths of the H.R.Gs built is a tribute to the toughness of the cars themselves and also to the great success of the H.R.G. Association. This club is celebrating its Silver Jubilee in the year of the publication of this book. It was founded in 1960 by Ian Dussek and Ron Knight (Brian Symes could not make that first meeting) and still exists today much in the same autocratic form as it started. Ian Dussek is still its secretary and historian. The club only accepts owners into membership though it does occasionally invite famous or notorious previous H.R.G. owners as associates. It runs a spares service which must be the envy of most one-make clubs: the service, I am told, is run very much on the lines of the factory, the spares even being kept in ex-works boxes. At the works, you were offered a cup of tea when you called for spares — the Association does the same!

The H.R.G. became a 'lost cause' about the time that the late Michael Sedgwick was so diligently researching Lord Montagu's books *Lost Causes of Motoring*. There was always a good attendance of H.R.Gs at 'Lost Causes' rallies in the 1960s at Beaulieu. One of my most enjoyable days out from the Museum office was in 1967 when Sedgwick and I went over to Kent to meet Ian Dussek and talk H.R.Gs for the day — the end product being a typically thorough article on the make from the pen of Michael Sedgwick, reproduced in *Veteran and Vintage* magazine in August 1967. Even though Michael had great difficulty in fitting behind the wheel of the H.R.G, I know that he had a great affection for the car and would I am sure be pleased to know that this important marque now has a published history and that it has only been made possible through the Trust which has been set up to honour his name by helping new and original research.

H.R.Gs by their very nature attracted strange and often eccentric people, so the stories about them are numerous. Ian Dussek tells me that he had a few problems with his editor who wanted to cut out some of the more scurrilous or rude stories. I am pleased that the editor was overruled and that many of them remain.

I have known Ian Dussek since school days: I was very soon aware of his interest in the H.R.G. and have seen the very enthusiastic way in which he has run the H.R.G. Association. All along he has been painstakingly collecting together facts about the make, but only now has he been able to put these facts down in book form. Michael Sedgwick wrote in his introduction to the *Veteran and Vintage* article that the H.R.G. was '. . . a sort of automotive coelacanth, surrounded by legend' – I am delighted the legend of the H.R.G. has now been told in full.

Michael E. Ware

Beaulieu
September 1985

Introduction

The Sportsman's Ideal — a rather ambitious claim for any sports car, but the one carried on H.R.G. literature and advertisements during their 31-year history. The justification is simple: the car, as built, could be driven to the office on a Friday, it could be driven to and raced at a racing circuit the following day, then rallied overnight. Subject to the stamina of the owner, it could be trialled on the Sunday. On Monday morning it could be driven back to the office, all without any spares or alterations other than those carried on the car. Not only was it rugged enough to take part in all these events, it could — and did — win.

The following pages feature individual cars which have competed in the Monte Carlo Rally and Les Vingt Quatre Heures du Mans in the same year, cars which have been equally successful in the Land's End Trial and the Alpine Rally. They were seldom the fastest but they finished, sometimes due to the determination of their drivers but basically due to the sound engineering principles employed in their design and construction. They were very safe cars and, despite some horrendous escapades, a very large proportion of the 241-odd cars which left the factory at Tolworth still survive today.

They are also among the most beautiful sports cars ever built, perfect examples of practical utility and sporting style. They have never received the recognition they so thoroughly deserved: hopefully, this book may help to rectify that in a small way. There may be other cars with an equal claim, but none greater than the H.R.G, to be 'The Sportsman's Ideal'.

Identification: where possible, I have referred to each individual car by its original United Kingdom registration number. Sometimes this is not possible, as in the case of the American cars, and there I have used the chassis number. The reason is two-fold: firstly, the chassis number is seldom, if ever, seen, certainly not on photographs, and is thus rather academic. Secondly, such information tends to create rather than solve disagreements — this book is not written with that in mind. For those who *are* interested in the chassis numbers, I have tried to explain how the numbering system worked.

Explanation: throughout the narrative, I have used the proper name H.R.G. Amongst owners and enthusiasts the make is affectionately known as the 'Hurg' (the 'g' is hard), and I have it on the best authority that the 'Hurg' is female: *It's a woman. Men rave about it in their earlier acquaintance days, tolerate and get used to its ways as time goes on and even when they part company it still occupies a special place and may return as the years go by.* (Letter from the Directors, 1961.)

Illustrations: most of the photographs have come from my own collection and from the archives of the H.R.G. Association. Others have been provided by the photographic library of the National Motor Museum and by a large number of kind individuals.

The illustrations at the head of each chapter were drawn by 'Arthur' Yarburgh-Bateson, Lord Deramore.Most of them were produced for the company and used as their Christmas Cards.

Acknowledgements: Grace Leather checked, amended and corrected my manuscript. She provided a considerable amount of hitherto unknown and invaluable information on the H.R.G. Engineering Company Limited with which she was so closely associated for thirty years. Without her help the writing of this book would have been impossible.

The Michael Sedgwick Memorial Trust

provided the impetus for the book and my thanks go to Michael Ware whose faith in this production has, I trust, been justified.

The editors of *Motor Sport, Autocar, Motor* and *Autosport* have kindly allowed me to use material from their publications. The National Motor Museum and the following individuals have provided encouragement, information and enthusiastic support –

Ray Barrington Brock	Alan Jenner
Neill Bruce	Louis Klemantaski
Marcus Chambers	Ian Mahany
Peter Clark	Tom Melahn
Lord Deramore	Cyril Posthumus
Roger Ericson	Guy Robins
Gary Ford	Brian Symes
Kyell Geijbrandt	Eric Thompson
Tim Jackson-Stops	Michael Usher
Jack Jarrett	Roger Williams

– and Kay Dorogsághy, who rendered my manuscript legible.

In conclusion — I grew up in a Lagonda family. Shortly after my 21st Birthday, I set out to buy a very special one which had once belonged to my godfather, a famous prewar driver. Alas, its condition had deteriorated beyond the resources of my meagre pocket and the purchase was not effected. That evening, an acquaintance offered me his 1100, thus beginning a quarter of a century's association with the marque H.R.G. I have never regretted it, and I hope some of the enthusiasm which I have for these magnificent cars permeates through the pages which follow.

Ian Dussek

Godfrey in action in his G.N. 'Bluebottle' at Tring in 1921. He retained a G.N. until the end of his life, although he had retired from active motor sport by the time the H.R.G. was launched (National Motor Museum).

Progenitors. The G.N. team for the 200 Mile Race at Brooklands in 1922. The drivers, left to right, are Hawkins, Frazer-Nash and Godfrey (National Motor Museum).

G.N. and after 1

1935-1936

When Archie Frazer-Nash and Ron Godfrey parted company with the ailing G.N. Motors Ltd in 1922, it was inconceivable that either of these motoring pioneers would be away from the motor manufacturing business for long. Frazer-Nash's immediate return and subsequent career have been painstakingly chronicled and the cars which bear his name have become world famous. Ron Godfrey's re-emergence, however, was to be delayed by over a decade and it may be said that in consequence the cars which bear his initials have never received the acclaim which they deserve. Perhaps what follows will help to put the record straight.

By 1923, the motor industry was undergoing the first of a number of crises which marked the inter-war years, and the new directors of G.N. Motors, along with many others, had lost their way trying to turn sporting cyclecars into suburban saloons. Both Godfrey and Nash had completely lost faith in the 'new money' and left them to get on with it. Sure enough, the G.N. was one of the casualties, along with such names as Calthorpe and Palladium.

Following a severe illness, Godfrey set up on his own account, servicing and preparing G.N. cars, of which several thousand had been produced both in England and, under licence, in France. H.R. Godfrey Motors, operating from Vitesse Works, Manor Road, Richmond, Surrey, offered a complete service, under 'the personal supervision of H.R. Godfrey'. Significantly, spares were offered at 'reduced prices', Godfrey having regarded the G.N. standard price schedule with some disfavour on account of the healthy mark-up. Special fittings, such as OHV cylinder head sets and improved safety hubcaps, were also catalogued, as were complete rebuilds based on the 1920-22 chassis, the end product being sold with a new-car guarantee.

Later, he teamed up with an old acquaintance from the days when he and Frazer-Nash had been studying for their City and Guilds in mechanical engineering before joining Willans and Robinson in Rugby. Stuart Proctor, whose background was in aeronautical engineering, joined him to form Godfrey and Proctor Ltd, still servicing G.Ns. Between times they constructed the 'Godfrey and Proctor', a vehicle combining the G.N. chassis and an Austin Seven engine, but it did not get further than a prototype. Not that all Ron Godfrey's interests were in cars: he had constructed his first motorcycle at the turn of the century and built up and maintained a collection of mediaeval English clocks.

Cars, though, were his major concern, with the accent very much on motor sport, and this of course led him to Brooklands, the focus of racing activity in prewar Britain.

In the early 1930s, Godfrey had become a leading member of the Junior Car Club and was much in evidence at Brooklands in an official capacity, including the job of scrutineer. The Light Car Club ran an International Relay Race at the track: teams of three cars competed over a total of 90 laps. One team included Jack Tuson in a Fiat and a G.N. driven by a retired major, Edward 'Ted' Athelstan Halford. After he had left the Army in 1930, Halford had bought a motor business in north London, acquiring a derelict G.N. which he had rebuilt and was racing. When the others in the team ran into mechanical problems during the race, Halford was called upon to drive for rather more than his allotted 30 laps, which he did with such enthusiasm that Godfrey, as chief scrutineer, was approached by worried fellow officials inquiring whether the frail-looking car was in fact safe. As co-designer of the G.N. he pronounced it was — and hoped for the best.

The contact made then was resumed later, Ted Halford having taken up a directorship with the Vale company, where he acted as designer. The Vale Special was a small sports car built at Maida Vale in London using Triumph and later Coventry-Climax engines: just over 100 Vales were built between 1932 and 1936. Following a visit to the Vale works, Godfrey approached Ted Halford about a project he had in mind, the production of a new sports car. Halford jumped at the chance, believing that a new car with Godfrey's reputation behind it offered greater prospects than Vales could provide. He gave his notice in forthwith, conveniently bringing with him a small legacy from a recently deceased relative.

The third member of the group was to be Guy Robins, another contact from the International Relay team, being a close friend of Jack Tuson. Guy was at the time in the design department of the Trojan company at Croydon, which produced rather more mundane transport than Godfrey proposed.

Following many discussions, a partnership between Halford, Robins and Godfrey was established in February 1935, and a garage workshop at the Mid-Surrey Gear Company, Hampden Road, Norbiton, was rented. The partners jointly designed and built the prototype car, with the

The prototype 1½-litre H.R.G. under construction at Norbiton in 1935. The temporary wooden former indicates the start of the body building phase.

assistance of one extra mechanic, Fred Mead, who remained with the organization for the next 20 years.

The concept of the new car was conservative and traditional, and in almost every respect swimming against the tide of sports car (and sporty car) design. By 1935, many sporting manufacturers had sacrificed performance to styling: bodies were increasing in weight, suspensions were slackened to ease the ride, and steering ratios were lowered for the benefit of the weak-wristed. In certain instances, the design team's whole idea of a sports car appeared to be a combination of aero screens, chrome mesh over the headlamps and wire wheels. In other words, what a later age would come to call the image was beginning to take precedence over what the engineer or the real enthusiast might want.

Not so the brainchild of Halford, Robins and Godfrey. For them, function was still the principal and, indeed, almost the only concern. The design involved low overall weight (1,570lb), with a 1½-litre engine, producing around 50bhp at moderate revs, thus enabling a comparatively high-ratio rear axle to be used. The engine was set well back in a robust but flexible chassis, using a deep, E-section channel frame. Wide springs helped to produce the necessary rigidity. The layout was tailored for good handling with a low centre of gravity and carefully designed steering geometry. A low unsprung weight was achieved by the design of the tubular front axle and enhanced by extremely light, 11in diameter magnesium alloy brake drums.

A large number of chassis parts were designed and fabricated on the partners' lathe, but the major items of the drive train were bought out, notably the Meadows 4ED Brooklands engine, Moss four-speed 'crash' gearbox, ENV spiral-bevel rear axle and Rudge centre-lock wheels. The steering box was Marles Weller and the chassis sidemembers were produced specially by Rubery Owen. The principal item of expense was the engine, which cost £34, but much money was saved by the sheer hard work of the partners: Ted Halford recalls working stripped to the waist 14 hours a day, seven days a week.

13

In due course, an ash-and-aluminium body with exposed slab tank was built up by Guy Robins more or less single-handed, and by the end of June 1935, the car was sufficiently advanced for the first rumours to start circulating in the press. These even included suggestions of an 1100 version, which did not materialize for another three years.

The new car was completed in under six months and, after a period of intensive testing, was announced to the world in November 1935. It was to be called the H.R.G, the initials of the three partners and also by happy coincidence those of Henry Ronald Godfrey and Guy Herbert Robins. The radiator badge and trademark consisted of the three initials set in a 48-beam sun ray, framed in an irregular octagon. The original colour scheme had the letters in scarlet and the rays in blue, but the design was subsequently improved aesthetically by being enamelled solely in black.

The details of the car had been most carefully thought out, giving a combination of exciting performance, precise handling, ease of accessibility and, above all, a feeling of fun. The response was immediate and favourable. *The Light Car* reported that each car would carry a certificate to the effect that it had been timed over the flying quarter-mile at no less than 90mph and it confirmed that the prototype, which was registered DPA 233, had achieved a standing quarter-mile time of 20 seconds on test. *The Light Car* also commented that the H.R.G. would present a considerable temptation to enthusiasts with moderate means but rather ambitious ideas on the subject of performance. *The Autocar* enthused on its exceptional roadholding qualities, combined with very good acceleration, advising that the car would be in production as soon as manufacturing arrangements were completed.

There was a clearly defined segment of the sports car market open to the

Engine compartment of the prototype, offside. The magneto is mounted across the front of the engine, with the advance and retard linkage coupled to a control rod running up through the steering box and column (The Autocar).

Engine compartment of the prototype, nearside. The exhaust manifold was later improved. The occupants' feet on the early cars were less than fully protected as the bonnet louvres continued past the bulkhead (The Autocar).

H.R.G, which was announced with the provisional price tag of £375. Further up the price list, the hand-built and highly competitive 1½-litre Aston Martins and Frazer-Nashes were selling at around £600-£700. At the other end, the MG PB, Singer Le Mans and Hillman Aero Minx could be bought for little more than £200. The 1½-litre British Salmson was selling at £395, but though its engine developed 70bhp, at over 2,400lb its potential performance was somewhat handicapped.

The H.R.G. Engineering Company formally registered the car with the Society of Motor Manufacturers and Traders on January 1, 1936. In the meantime, plans for production were well advanced. Godfrey had organized the purchase of a plot of land at Oakcroft Road, a new industrial estate just off the Kingston By-Pass at Chessington, Surrey, in conjunction with his old friend Archie Frazer-Nash, whose company — Nash and Thompson — took a neighbouring plot. On February 22, 1936, the H.R.G. Engineering Co Ltd was established, with a capital of £1,000 and with a London solicitor, Richard Churchill, as Chairman. Introduced through Hywell Murrell, a friend of Robins, Churchill was able to organize the necessary financial backing for the new venture in the form of redeemable debentures from the funds of the shipping magnate and recluse, Sir John Ellerman.

The Limited Company began to operate at Oakcroft Road with Halford designated as Company Secretary and Office and Sales Manager, Robins as Works Director and Godfrey as Designer and Technical Director. Robins brought in David Eadington for the machine and toolroom operations, together with George Talbot for welding and sheet metal work. The two had been with Robins at Trojan, but Talbot had set up on his own and had carried out the welding work on the prototype. So the company started with a toolmaker and a welder, plus Fred Mead as fitter, together with an odd job man, Skelton, who had also helped at Norbiton. At that time, the basic rates for toolmaker/turners were 1s 8d per hour and for fitters 1s 6d, working a 5½-day, 48-hour week. The shop boy, taken on after a few months, was paid 4d per hour.

It soon became obvious that Halford could not cope with all the typing and office work, so when Grace Leather, who lived nearby, approached Godfrey for employment, it was suggested she should undertake some

Cockpit of the prototype. The steering wheel boss carries advance/retard and slow-running levers. Hidden to its right are the oil pressure and water temperature gauges: the dial on the extreme left shows oil temperature (The Autocar).

The Oakcroft Road factory, seen here when newly built. The office window in the upper part of the front wall is in the form of the H.R.G. trademark.

The scene inside the new factory with the prototype receiving attention. Visible on the left are some of the power tools driven by belt from an overhead lineshaft.

The first batch of three chassis laid out in the factory. In the background Guy Robins is deep in thought while nearer the camera a new Meadows engine awaits installation.

typing of sales letters in the evenings and at weekends. This continued for some months, using the company's portable typewriter, which was left with the necessary papers in a shed at the rear of the works. In September, she took on fulltime employment as a clerk-typist and general dogsbody, thus beginning 30 years with the company.

Within the first two years, the workforce had increased to 10, including Doug Orchard and Bill Constable, who had been at AFN Ltd with Fred Mead. Pat Evendon, the company's first apprentice, was taken on and was joined by Ken Baillie Hill and J. Eric West. They all paid premiums, and were essentially employed on car production, whereas later apprentices were indentured and covered by a modified version of the standard Engineering Federation apprenticeship contract. Baillie Hill helped build his own car, GPB 250, whilst at the works and West also owned one. From the start it was intended to utilize any spare capacity by undertaking subcontract engineering work, which Robins was very successful in obtaining. General engineering soon represented nearly a quarter of the company's sales.

First racing outing for the marque. Curtis, in company with heavier metal, at the October Brooklands meeting in 1936.

The interest the prototype car created continued and in fact increased, but sales were not materializing in the numbers hoped for, so it was thought a salesman would be a worthwhile recruit. As a result, another friend of Robins, Anthony Curtis, joined the company on the basis of a small salary and commission. He was full of enthusiasm and ideas, with some managerial acumen, being a director of the Grand Union Canal Co Ltd and a City property company, besides being Honorary Secretary of the Light Car Club.

The car was now being entered in various competitions and Robins won the first trophy, a second-class award, at the JCC Driving Tests in February 1936, where he caught the attention of the reporters and drew very favourable comments on the acceleration and braking. On the Land's End Trial at Easter, Robins took the first of a very long list of MCC premier awards. By June, there was an order book, with VSCC founder-member Harold Powell at the top of the list, and by the end of 1936 five production models had been completed. The marque was on its way.

The H.R.G.

2

Technical appreciation

There can be few marques that have remained so apparently unchanged for such a long period as H.R.G. Changes there were but, setting aside the later twin-cam project, the overall concept for almost all the cars remained unaltered over a period of 20 years. And even that is not the whole story, since the car launched in 1935 drew much of its inspiration from the G.N. of the 1920s. Comparison of the outline specifications of the H.R.G. 1100 of 1939 and the Touring model G.N. of 1920, in the accompanying table, makes interesting reading. The similarities are remarkable and yet the G.N, which was no mean performer in its day, was classified as a cyclecar whereas the H.R.G. was definitely a thoroughbred sports car. Perhaps, therefore, there is an answer to W.H. Charnock's famous question —

'Nash and Godfrey hated cogs,
Built a car with chains and dogs.
It worked — but would it if
They had made it with a diff?'

It did, and it was called an H.R.G! Continuing development and accumulated experience carried on from the G.N. to the H.R.G. improved the basic design in detail and confirmed how fundamentally right it was from the start.

To see just how the H.R.G's qualities were achieved requires a study of the technical attributes of the car. In laying down the original design Godfrey set certain objectives:

1   To build a light car. This is known to be the cheapest way of attaining performance.
2   To build a reliable car, something not altogether achieved in previous light designs.

3 To build a simple car, thus achieving ease of maintenance and repair.
4 To build a quality product, without the necessity for high expenditure.

The mechanical layout followed the classic pattern well tried and proven through the development of vintage sports cars. The front axle was forward of the radiator and the conventionally placed 'north-south' engine and gearbox drove the rear axle via a propeller shaft. This differed from G.N. practice where belts or chains had been used. With a wheel at each corner, stiff, well-damped suspension and the concentration of weight towards the centre of the car, the chassis made for good handling and roadholding characteristics. To ensure full advantage was taken of this layout a simple yet clever method of construction was designed. In brief, the H.R.G. adopted the best in traditional sports-car practice but made use of modern engineering techniques such as rubber bushes and mountings to achieve improved performance and simplicity.

	G. N. (1920)	H.R.G. 1100 (1939)
Wheelbase	8ft 6in	8ft 3½in
Track	3ft 6in	F: 4ft 0in, R: 3ft 9in
Overall length	11ft 5in	11ft 10½in
Overall width	4ft 5in	4ft 7in
Front suspension	Quarter-elliptic	Quarter-elliptic
Rear suspension	Half-elliptic	Half-elliptic
Engine capacity	1,087cc	1,074cc
Power output	20bhp	38bhp
Top gear ratio	4:1	4.55:1 (4:1 optional)
Weight	952 lb	1,540 lb
Power to weight ratio	47.1bhp/ton	55.3bhp/ton

The description of the component parts and types of H.R.G. which follows, notwithstanding the broad lack of change, is to some extent a generalization. H.R.Gs were hand-built cars, constructed to the whims of the customers and the necessities of the factory. That one postwar 1500 had an exposed slab tank means that the customer wanted it that way. That the chassis rail of one car has two chassis numbers is the result of some major surgery following an accident. So what follows is a practical working guide, not definitive to the last nut and bolt.

The chassis
The heart of the H.R.G. is its chassis and the progression of types and numbers is important to students of the marque. The prototype and first production models had numbers prefixed with the letter A, the prototype being numbered A50. Although some small changes were made in the early days, the numbering ran on to A65, at which point the chassis was widened by 3 inches. Numbers which followed were thus wide chassis, or W, running from W66 on to W221 in 1952. Both Meadows and Singer-based engines were installed in the W series chassis, but, when it came to the installation of the short-stroke Singer SM Hunter engine, minor modifications were necessary and the last chassis — from 1953 to 1956 — were classified WS and numbered from 222 to 233.

All the A, W and WS chassis were for the 1½-litre engines, Meadows or

Tail of the 1½-litre in production form. The inner line of the rear wing has been smoothed out in comparison with the proto-type, and the doors are now front-hinged.

Singer. The 1100 chassis was virtually identical, but 3½ inches shorter in the wheelbase, the difference being in the engine section. The 1100s were prefixed S, commencing at S50 and running to S98.

Left-hand-drive versions were given an extra prefix L, eg L/W143, but a left-hand-drive number did not necessarily mean that the car ended up with left-hand drive — it merely indicated that when the chassis was laid down the intention was to build it with left-hand steering. One customer changed his mind no less than three times while his car was in production.

Perhaps surprisingly, the Aerodynamic 1500s carried no special chassis identification. Although at first glance there were several modifications, such as a subframe over the front axle, and the fittings to hold the spare wheel and the fuel tank on the outside of the sidemembers, these were all extra to the basic chassis rather than modifications and all were removable. Given a limited number of replacement parts, a new body, time and money, an Aerodynamic could become a standard two-seater.

One other chassis number prefix exists: the frame for the sole prewar coupe, which had a Triumph engine, was given the identification W/T68.

In its construction, the chassis frame itself was of the classic 'ladder' type. The two channel-section parallel sidemembers were joined by four main crossmembers and, to achieve simplicity and ease of maintenance, bolts were the principal method of securing. Right at the front, a fully-boxed crossmember carried the radiator and helped to feed front suspension loads into the frame. Halfway back a 2¾in diameter tubular crossmember was bolted in through flanges welded to the tube ends and this controlled the torsional stress between the two sidemembers. Two 1½in diameter tubular crossmembers at the rear of the chassis were extended through the sidemembers to locate the wide-based rear springs, with the rearmost one pinned in position through cast lugs welded to the sidemember ends.

The sidemembers themselves were 4⅛in deep, forming a strong yet light bridge between the axles. They were shaped and tapered at the rear to drop under the rear axle but were otherwise straight, making the frame simple and uniform. Compared to a similar MG chassis, the sidemembers were much deeper but of thinner material, resulting in a light construction — light enough to be carried by an able-bodied person — easily repaired should the need arise.

At the front, the sidemember flanges were widened to meet the boxed crossmember and carried the engine mountings on Singer-engined cars. A minor crossmember of E-section was fitted to support the gearbox and just aft of the centre tube a brake cross-shaft was mounted, running in cast housings fitted with needle rollers. The sidemembers were formed by Rubery Owen to H.R.G. design, while the crossmembers were made by H.R.G, who used jigs for welding and drilling all these components.

Originally, thinner gauge sidemembers were supplied in error, but the correct $^7/_{64}$in (12 gauge) gave a good compromise between lightness and strength. All frames of this traditional type were made to flex and work with the suspension media to achieve the desired ride and roadholding capabilities. The H.R.G. was no exception to this, but was made to be strong and rigid where it mattered to produce above-average steering and handling. In normal use frames lasted well, but in extreme competition situations weaknesses did show up. The main stress points were around the steering box mounting and just in front of the bolted sideplates supporting the bulkhead and main body frame. Where fractures occurred the repaired chassis were fitted with flitch plates running through the damaged areas inside the channel sidemembers. This not only achieved a stronger frame, but also improved the steering. Some cars bear the scars of competition or accident damage and a few sidemembers have been repaired by welding a section into them, thus demonstrating the ease of repair.

Cockpit of the 1½-litre, with the Moss gearbox and gearchange assembly visible. The clutch and brake pedal pads were later cast in the shape of the company's trademark, replacing the circular pattern fitted to this car.

22

Front axle and suspension

To achieve good handling, a low centre of gravity is desirable and many vintage-style cars obtained this with complex frame shapes which were expensive and difficult to produce and repair, the sidemembers arching over the axles. At the front of the car, the H.R.G. achieved a low build by virtually having the chassis chopped off at the rear mounting of the quarter-elliptic springs. The front springs were then bolted to the chassis direct and extended forward in line with the sidemembers. The tail of the spring had a bolt through it and a U-bolt passed over the spring through the front boxed crossmember to stop lateral movement. This U-bolt also secured the base of the headlamp and front wing mounting bar.

The generously proportioned quarter-elliptic springs were 18in long with seven $\frac{7}{32}$in thick leaves. One weakness of the design was the narrow spring base and to obtain good roll resistance the springs had to be stiff and were set to flatten at 220lb load. This may well be one reason why the chassis design was widened early in the history of the car, thus putting the springs further apart and improving the roll stiffness and control. Underneath each road spring was an H.R.G-designed adjustable friction shock absorber, each one having four friction pads, with the body secured to the chassis via the tail of the U-bolt securing the spring. The arms of the shock absorbers extended forward and the front axle flanges were fixed to the springs and shocker arms using bolts through maintenance-free Silentbloc bushes. Steering castor angle was regulated by an adjustable knuckle on the shock absorber arm.

This simple and clever system meant the axle was rigidly secured to the car against sideways forces generated by cornering and twisting forces created under braking; also, castor angles remained constant during suspension movement. Such a high degree of axle control was seldom found on production cars employing beam axles with shackled road springs. On the other hand, removal of the front axle assembly meant merely undoing four bolts, removing two brake pins, and separating a steering joint, after which the axle could be rolled away.

The front axle itself was ingenious in design, achieving a light assembly which was extremely strong: it consisted of three main parts. The centre section was a length of seamless steel tube, $2\frac{1}{8}$in diameter outside and $\frac{1}{8}$in

Bare H.R.G. chassis with the front springs fitted. There are six body mounting points, two at the rear and two on each side of the chassis to the rear of the prominent vertical firewall supports.

23

Rolling chassis of a 1500. Clearly visible in this view is the way in which the rear ends of the rear springs slide through slots in the rear spring bearer tube, providing more positive location than swinging shackles.

thick, to which the suspension flanges were jig welded at an angle. The ends of this tube were then bored inside with a fine taper. The two outer ends of the axle were forgings machined to shape, hollowed out and bored at rightangles to accept the kingpins. The inboard ends were fine tapered to fit the centre tube and were pressed into the tube in the correct position, then secured by taper pins.

The straight, hollow beam was now bent at the centre using a jig, thus bringing the pairs of suspension flanges parallel to each other and producing kingpin inclination to achieve centre-point steering. Bending the axle also helped to make the car lower and allowed the entry of the starting handle, unimpeded by the axle beam.

In operation, the use of steep castor and kingpin angles helped to keep the outside wheel square to the road, maximizing grip and producing good 'feel' for the driver.

Rear axle and suspension
The rear axle and suspension layout followed more conventional patterns and the axle itself appeared overweight for a car where weight-saving was high on the list of priorities. However, high strength and reliability were being sought, thus allowing for future power increases.

Semi-elliptic leaf springs were used which were 39in long and had seven leaves, each $\frac{7}{32}$in thick and $1\frac{3}{4}$in wide. Some cars were fitted with nine thinner leaves, but both types had a 330lb load rating to set flat. The front was secured on the extended crossmember via a Silentbloc bush set into the spring eye. At the rear, the main leaf slid through the rear crossmember, running in hardened steel trunnions. This system minimized any sideways float or play by eliminating shackles and the substantial size of the springs controlled the axle well even under hard accelerating and braking torque loads.

Damping of these springs was important, particularly as they carried the majority of the weight of the vehicle. Initially, a choice of H.R.G. friction or Luvax hydraulic piston dampers was offered. Later, the two types were

This W series chassis is ready for delivery to Fox & Nicholl to have an Aerodynamic body fitted and has the front subframe and special radiator designed to accommodate the all-enveloping style coach-work (The Motor).

fitted together, thus offering the advantages of both, although for normal road use the hydraulic system usually provided sufficient control on its own. These shock absorbers were secured forward and behind the axle and were coupled to the bottom spring clamping plate. The axle casing rested on the springs, located by a rivet head set into each spring saddle. Twin U-bolts passed over each side of the axle and through the bottom clamping plate where nuts secured them and clamped the spring tightly.

Bump stops were fitted in the form of hoops over the axle casing on each side, but these were rarely needed except in extreme conditions, such as trials, and the car did not suffer from wheel lifting or axle tramp under hard cornering. While the front springs supported a fairly constant load, the rear springs carried virtually all the variable weight of petrol, luggage and occupants. Consequently, they worked hard and could sometimes lose their camber with age. Any spring maker could rectify this state by resetting the spring to $3\frac{1}{2}$in to 4in free camber. When the car was standing unladen the spring had about 1in positive camber for best results.

The rear axles were made by ENV, who supplied many car makers with axles and gearboxes before the war. Type A165 was used and had a conventional differential unit. Four final-drive ratios were available, 5:1, 4.55:1, 4:1 and 3.7:1. The three lower-geared versions had spiral-bevel crownwheel-and-pinion assemblies, while the 3.7:1 unit had weaker, straight-cut gears. Generally, 4.55:1 and 4:1 ratios were supplied as standard on 1100 and 1500 models respectively. The axle was well capable of handling the power of standard H.R.G. engines and was very trouble-free. Replacement of pinion bearings and the tightening of crownwheel nuts was recommended on old, well-used examples, and the use of the correct 140 SAE oil was essential.

The substantial halfshafts went out to three-quarter-floating hub assemblies supported by large, double-track ball races. The Rudge Whitworth splined wheel hubs tapered on to the halfshafts with drive keys and retaining nuts. These nuts had to be kept tight and usually the weakest link in the axle was this keyed hub taper. Normally, if damage was not too great, a replacement key fixed things again and this was preferable to breaking the shafts. The later SM Singer-engined cars adopted a Salisbury axle, with a ratio of 4.1:1, similar to that used on Jaguar and Morgan cars and, if anything, this unit was even more robust.

Steering

One of the features of the H.R.G. was the steering, which was light and direct with plenty of 'feel'. The system gave the driver confidence that the car would go where it was asked and, particularly on a smooth road, these steering qualities are hard to match on production cars today.

In the cockpit, the driver was faced with a 17in diameter (large by modern standards) Dover four-spoke sprung steering wheel on a column which was adjustable in height at the mounting of the steering box to suit individual requirements.

Earlier cars were fitted with a Marles worm-and-peg type steering box with a ratio of $1\frac{5}{8}$ turns lock-to-lock for a 32ft turning circle. Later cars had a lighter Marles worm-and-wheel unit first used on the 1100 in 1938 and then standard on all models. This 320-type box was probably a bit too light and was not as strong as the original assembly, but providing the box and its support were maintained properly, reasonable service life resulted. In recent years, due to lack of availability of spares, the Marles type 426 box has been modified for use. This is much more robust altogether, although space is rather limited in the engine bay.

The steering box was supported high on the chassis sidemember by an alloy stanchion nicknamed 'the lighthouse' because of its shape. This clamped the box about the cross-shaft housing and a drop arm was fitted on the outside of the car which picked up the fore-and-aft drag link to the

The front suspension, showing the kingpin and stub axle assembly pinned to the axle tube which is located by the front spring and shock absorber arm. The drag link, steering arm and track rod are also visible.

front axle. As the axle was rigidly secured in a fore-and-aft direction, the resultant forces acted very directly without play or float and this ensured the accurate steering which the car possessed.

This side view of the 1500 works demonstrator MPG 177 illustrates clearly the classic profile of the car, simple, functional and harmoniously well-proportioned. The built-in petrol tank results in an uncluttered line at the rear.

Wheels, tyres and brakes

Rudge centre-lock wheels were standard wear for all models. Two basic tyre sizes — 4.75 x 17 and 5.50 x 16 — were normally fitted, with Dunlop for preference. In general, 17in rims were used prior to 1948 and 16in thereafter, but there were many variants. Some cars were supplied with both, even to the extent of a 16in car carrying two 17in spares (which made mending a puncture a major operation). The reason was that the car could be used in competition with either size to suit conditions on the spur of the moment. The Aerodynamic carried its single spare inboard, but the open two-seaters were supplied with single or twin rear-mounted spares.

The change to a wider tyre perhaps forecast the modern trend towards lower-profile, wider tyres — for touring purposes the 5.50 x 16 tyres certainly gave a more comfortable ride. At a time when narrow tyres running at high pressures were common, H.R.G. found that a lightly-laden, wider tyre could be run at lower pressures and 16psi was quoted for road use on the 16in tyre. The maximum load rating of this size of tyre was 895lb, giving the car a tyre capacity of nearly 3,600lb. For a car weighing 1,700lb the tyres were clearly not overworked, resulting in excellent wear properties as well as further enhancement of roadholding qualities from the increased contact with the road.

The cockpit of MPG 177 shows the 1500's well-stocked dashboard. Between the speedometer and rev counter (with clock) are an ammeter and gauges for fuel level, oil pressure, oil temperature, water temperature and manifold vacuum. The slender steering wheel is free of controls.

A vital element in obtaining the best from any sporting car is the braking. Until the advent of the hydraulic-braked WS cars, the system originally adopted was the same for all models. A simple cable layout was used with separate individually-adjusted cables running from a centrally-placed cross-shaft to each brake. The cables were the Bowden type with an outer casing anchored to the chassis at one end and to the brake backplate at the other, and the inner cable running through it.

The basic brake operated on the fixed pivot principle with the shoes securely pinned at one end and moved by the cable-operated cam at the other, but also fixed in an accurately-bushed housing. Although at first sight it looked like a one-leading-one-trailing system, the absence of any float meant that no self-servo action took place, so each shoe made the same braking contribution, the system worked with equal effect either forwards or backwards, and the lining wear rate was even on each shoe.

The backplates and covers were all made of aluminium and the 11in diameter drums were cast in magnesium alloy with cast-iron liners shrunk and pinned in position. Each drum had a large, single strengthening rib outside and was extremely rigid and light. The shoes themselves were also of light alloy and the saving in unsprung weight was considerable. The $1\frac{1}{4}$in wide linings were rivetted in place and were of Ferodo MZ 41 material.

An unusual feature in the cockpit was the brake adjuster in front of the driver's seat. This adjusted the brake pedal free travel under repeated heavy braking conditions as the alloy drums tended to expand more than most and pedal movement could become excessive. One had to remember to back the adjuster off again after usage because cooling of the drums could sometimes result in the brakes locking on.

All WS-series cars were fitted with a hydraulic system using the same basic drum and backplate, but having a twin-leading-shoe system on the front with self-servo action: proprietary steel shoes, suitably modified, with bonded linings were employed. Some earlier cars were modified to this system, which possessed considerably better performance.

The fly-off handbrake was positioned to the left of the gearlever. On cable-brake cars it operated via a link direct on to the cross-shaft thus using all four brakes, but on the hydraulic system only the rear brakes were operated by the handbrake. Best results were obtained by attention to detail, for example ensuring that all lever angles were correct, the mechanism was properly lubricated and the linings were properly bedded in.

In 1950, John Bolster tested a 1500 for *Autosport* and described the brakes like this: *The brakes have not the ultra-light pedal pressure that characterizes current hydraulic designs but they are powe:ful once one has become accustomed to this. I used them hard but did not succeed in making them fade, though they produced a strong smell of Ferodo when heavily applied at 90mph. (Autosport, October 6, 1950.)*

Engine

Initially, the 4ED Meadows engine was installed in the car. This engine was well-proven and had already powered other successful cars such as Frazer-Nash and Lea-Francis. By 1935 it was perhaps becoming rather dated, although when used in a light chassis the performance was still competitive. The bore and stroke measured 69mm x 100mm, giving a capacity of 1,496cc, and the overhead valves were operated by pushrods from a side-mounted, gear-driven camshaft. In standard 'big crank' Brooklands form some 58bhp was produced at 4,000rpm with a lusty torque curve producing good power from about 1,600rpm. Carburation was by two SUs and ignition was supplied by a Scintilla magneto and 18mm spark plugs.

While the radiator capacity of $2\frac{1}{2}$ gallons permitted thermosyphon cooling, later engines were fitted with water pumps. Owners soon found readily available methods of tuning these engines and cars sprouted improved exhaust manifolds and other modifications. Experiments were carried out on the cylinder heads and the H.R.G. Le Mans model was fitted for a time with the Gough deflector head. There is no doubt that the cars performed well enough one way or another. All the pre-1938 $1\frac{1}{2}$-litre H.R.Gs were fitted with 4ED units.

It was in 1938 that the H.R.G. name became linked with Singer and this combination is the best known. Indeed, the cars have sometimes been called 'Singer/H.R.G.' which implies that Singer played a major role in the vehicle. In fact, this was far from the truth, for although H.R.G. Engineering bought the basic engines from Singer, a great deal of development work was then carried out to increase the power output.

For ease of identification, it is usual to refer to the Meadows-engined cars as '$1\frac{1}{2}$-litre' and the 1,496cc Singer-engined cars as '1500'. There was no conscious factory decision to differentiate between the two, but the distinction is convenient. All the 1100 models were fitted with Singer units.

Initially, two engines were used, of the types which Singer fitted to their 9, 10, Super 10, 12 and Super 12 saloon models. Both engines employed chain-driven overhead camshafts operating inclined valves via L-shaped

Nearside of the 1500 engine showing the manifold arrangement and the water pump driven by the fanbelt. Two 6-volt batteries are set in a box above the scuttle.

rockers, with a combustion chamber of nicely rounded shape. They differed from the earlier Singer Le Mans engines in having robust, three-bearing crankshafts, but the overall design was again a well-proven one.

The change to Singer engines ensured a more guaranteed source of supply, particularly if sales were to increase. Technically, there were other advantages in adopting the more modern design and, although many claim that the Meadows cars were faster and more tunable, the Singer engines were far smoother, more refined and much easier to drive. It must be remembered that the faster Meadows cars had engines tuned to their limits in cars stripped of any excess weight.

Most of the H.R.G. work was concentrated on the more popular 1500 engine which replaced the Meadows 1½-litre. The Singer 12 engine was purchased complete and then stripped down by H.R.G. Engineering and rebuilt. The counterbalanced crankshaft was replaced by one with a 2mm-shorter stroke (103mm) to bring the capacity down from 1,525cc to 1,496cc, inside the 1,500cc classification for motor sport. Stronger big-end bolts were fitted and new solid-skirt pistons raised the compression ratio and allowed larger gudgeon pins to be used. Initially these pistons were supplied by Martlett and later by Hepworth & Grandage: at first, they raised the compression ratio from 6:1 to 7:1, later to 8:1.

To improve the breathing, further changes included a new camshaft operating larger inlet and domed exhaust valves with stronger double valve springs. Externally, a four-branch exhaust manifold and twin 1¼in carburettors helped to add further power and the addition of a water pump kept things cool. Inlet ports were enlarged and reshaped, the ignition timing modified and, once assembled, each engine was test-bench run to check settings and power output. H.R.G. developed various options for the engine, including a larger, aluminium oil sump to replace the pressed-steel one, a full-flow oil filter system and an oil cooler arrangement.

All these changes raised the power from 43bhp to between 61 and 66bhp without loss of reliability. Further attempts to raise the power could result

Offside of the 1500 engine, with Scintilla Vertex magneto fitted. Twin fuel pumps are mounted on the firewall and there are two horns on the front of the block under the header tank. The crudely beaten-out bulge in the side of the footwell on the left provides the driver with a little more foot room.

in problems, however, and this did limit the owners' ability to be competitive in later years of H.R.G. history. The principal weakness lay in the inability of the head gasket to cope with the heat between the siamesed bores of cylinders 1-2 and 3-4, where no cooling water passages were provided. The installation of lipped cylinders did nothing to help solve this problem, and the tortuous route of the exhaust gases across the cylinder head to the manifold also tended to heat things up more than was desirable. Even so, the car performed reliably on most occasions in all sorts of motor sporting events and much improved fuel economy was achieved compared with the Meadows-powered cars.

The 1100 engine went through similar treatment at the factory, but the cubic capacity, at 1,074cc, needed no alteration, so the Singer crankshaft was used. The engine was very similar to the 1500 and was fitted with twin 1⅛in SU carburettors to produce 38bhp at 4,000 rpm. This unit proved more reliable and more tunable than the 1500 and powered cars to many competition victories in its class. An enlarged, 1,188cc version was catalogued by the company, but one only was sold and the 1100 model remained in production through to 1950 with only minor alterations.

The long-stroke 12 was superseded by Singer early in 1949 and a new, much improved, shorter-stroke unit with bore and stroke measuring 73mm x 89.4mm, giving 1,497cc, was introduced. Designated the SM engine, it was fitted to the Hunter series of cars and developed some 56bhp in standard form. It was clearly an engine designed with future development in mind and although the low-speed torque was not quite as good, the power above 4,000 rpm was considerably better than the old 1500. At first H.R.G. made some modifications to the engine, fitting special Martlett pistons, but the last few to leave the factory were neat Singer with improved manifolding. All these went to the USA. The engine was far superior in every way, except that it weighed more, and certainly did not suffer the failings of its predecessor, although the cam and valve layout was the same.

The power units sat well back in the chassis frame and, whereas the

Detail of the 1500 engine compartment, offside. The steering box is clamped to its mounting by two long bolts passing through the chassis. The bypass oil filter is located to the rear of the chain-driven dynamo.

Meadows engine was bolted directly to the chassis, Singer engines were flexibly mounted at three points. This not only took full advantage of the superior smoothness of the Singer engines, but also allowed the frame to work better, avoiding additional stress-raisers in the sidemembers.

The transmission system

H.R.G cars used a traditional transmission system driven through a single-plate clutch with the gearbox bolted directly to the engine bellhousing. In turn, the gearbox drove an open propeller shaft with the usual universal joints at each end taking drive to the rear axle. The gearboxes were supplied as units from proprietary sources, but even so a wide variety of ratios was offered.

The Meadows engine was mated to a Moss 'crash'-type gearbox with straight-cut gears and a neat remote-control lever mounted in a vintage-style gear gate. By 'crash' box standards it was easy to use, although rather noisy in the indirect gears. The following ratios were standard:

Top	Direct
Third	1.39:1
Second	2.3:1
First	4.8:1
Reverse	4.89:1

The standard axle ratio of 4:1 gave an overall top gearing of 20mph/1,000 rpm and a useful third-gear speed of over 60mph. Other ratios were available for owners so their cars could be better suited for racing by having a closer set or for trials by employing lower first and second gears, for example.

With the change to Singer engines, it was logical to use the standard Singer gearbox which was more modern and had synchromesh on the top three gears, making it considerably easier to use. As it was also equipped with helical gearing (except on first) it was much quieter in the

32

intermediate gears than the old Moss box. Gearchanging was via a neat remote-control linkage with the lever working in a ball socket. Various-length remote controls were offered to suit the requirements of individual owners. Apart from shortening the gearlever, the only other alterations to the standard gearbox for fitting to the H.R.G. were modified layshaft bushes to improve lubrication.

In operation, the Singer box enabled fast gearchanges to be executed and the quietness of the second and third gears complemented the sophisticated feel of the engine. From a service point of view the unit was trouble-free, but age did eventually show up weaknesses including an irritating tendency to jump out of gear.

The 1500 and 1100 gearboxes were virtually identical. The earlier models used a four-stud mounting, later changing to a six-stud type. Standard ratios for both gearboxes were:

Top	Direct
Third	1.47:1
Second	2.27:1
First	3.59:1
Reverse	3.5:1

Compared to the Moss gearbox a higher first gear was noticeable, but when coupled to the 4:1 axle on the 1500, the overall top gearing remained at 20mph/1,000rpm, with a third-gear speed of nearly 70mph from the freer-revving engine. The 1100 axle of 4.55:1 ratio gave an overall top gearing of some 17.2 mph/1,000rpm.

A selection of alternative ratios was available: by changing the pair of input gears driving the layshaft, the first three gears could be made nearer in ratio to the direct top gear or further away, thus altering the usable speeds in the intermediate gears as well as the gap between third and top. A chart was supplied in the instruction manual showing how the alternative gearbox and axle ratios combined to affect speeds in the gears. Some idea of the choice of ratios offered to customers is given by the accompanying table which shows road speeds at 5,000rpm for one series of options.

		4:1 axle	3.7:1 axle	4.55:1 axle
Standard gearbox:	**Top**	100mph	108mph	88mph
	Third	68mph	74mph	60mph
Closer-ratio gearbox:	**Top**	100mph	108mph	88mph
	Third	80mph	86mph	69mph

At the back of the gearbox was a synthetic-rubber yoke arrangement which formed the single rear engine mounting and was bolted to a minor chassis crossmember. The later SM-engined cars used a very similar gearbox, but equipped with a stronger mainshaft, different ratios, and an extended rear cover.

Fuel and electrical systems
The early Meadows-engined cars were fitted with 15-gallon fuel tanks mounted vertically outside the rear of the body. By 1939 a square-sectioned tank was designed to fit just behind the rear axle and inside the body, which was extended to accommodate it. Although tank capacity was reduced to 10 gallons, the better fuel consumption of the Singer engines still allowed a useful range of 260 to 300 miles or so. An optional 12-gallon tank was available for long-distance rally events, and the Aerodynamic cars contained oval-shaped 11-gallon tanks.

Fuel was taken to the engine through a $5/16$in copper pipe by a bulkhead-mounted SU electric pump on the Meadows and 1500, or an AC mechanical pump on the 1100. Many of the $1\frac{1}{2}$-litre cars and 1500s were equipped with twin electric pumps individually switched and 1100s sometimes had both electric and mechanical pumps. These duplicated systems were used particularly on competition cars such as those driven on the Alpine rallies, which were also fitted with fuel filters because of previous experience with poor-quality fuel in postwar France.

All cars were equipped with a straightforward 12-volt electrical system. On the early cars battery fitment was two 6-volt units in series mounted at the rear, but later they were carried in the bulkhead tray. Meadows and 1500 engines drove their substantial dynamos from the camshaft drives, whereas the 1100 used the fanbelt.

The headlamps had foot-controlled dip systems which originally cut out the offside lamp. Most cars were later converted to double-dip systems with sealed-beam lights. Basically the electrical department proved to be very reliable and was essentially simple enough to retain a rebuildable quality even when original spare parts became impossible to obtain.

The body

The basic H.R.G. two-seater body remained fundamentally unaltered throughout the 21 years of production. However, there were many detail changes and refinements, culminating in a well thought-out and developed product. As with anything handmade, though, it is safe to say that no two H.R.G. bodies were identical. At the front, the flowed wings were mounted on the headlamp bar and curved down to a second mounting on the chassis sidemember. These wings were separate from the body itself and thus were easily changed for the cycle type or removed altogether for competition work.

The radiator was mounted behind the front axle and headlamp bar, giving a low, purposeful face to the car, and the radiator curves gave shape to the light aluminium bonnet. With the usual centre-hinge opening this bonnet, louvred at the sides, allowed easy access to the engine bay. A strong bulkhead structure supported the dashboard and steering column, allowing the car to be driven without the bodywork, which was fitted on separately. From the bulkhead to the rear of the car, the body frame was made in light, flexible ash rails over which aluminium panels were fitted. The rear wings screwed up to the integral wheelarches to finish the rear of the car. The body was mounted on rubber pads at the four outrigger

Dashboard of an 1100. The layout is similar to the 1500, but with a different pattern speedometer and rev counter, the latter lacking the inset clock of the other model. All the other dials are there, though.

brackets near the cockpit, and on the chassis at the rear. The front of this structure was bolted directly to the bulkhead, thus forming a rigid, shake-free scuttle assembly.

Initially, a top-mounted windscreen wiper mechanism was fitted, but this was soon altered to a bottom-mounted type, thus relieving the screen of stress and making the wipers more effective, particularly in snow. Many other detail refinements were made throughout the car as time went by including reshaping the windscreen, the radiator aperture and the front wings. Even the body rails themselves experienced detail curve alterations: but from the start the basic shape and character of the car had been set and needed no change.

The prewar 1½-litre bodies were built by Alban Croft of South Croydon. In 1938 production for the 1100 bodywork was negotiated with Reall, a large coachworks in West London, as substantial volume was envisaged. The Reall bodies were more sophisticated in detail and, as mentioned, the fuel tank was brought inboard, so, with the extended rear, the wings were built into the body more than attached to it. Reall also built many of the postwar bodies for the 1500, but by 1947 the work was being shared with Automarine Ltd, a small bodyworks at St Leonards, Sussex, who had taken on an ex-Reall employee, B.W. Locke. From the middle of 1948 only Automarine bodies were supplied. The two bodybuilders produced almost identical results, although Automarine's treatment of the rear wings appears more slender. Automarine changed its name to St Leonards Engineering Co in 1950, but did not prosper, so the last half-dozen cars were built to the special instructions of H.R.G. by two St Leonards employees, Arthur Rothon and Alan Jenner.

As with most quality cars of the time, the H.R.G. could be purchased in chassis form and contemporary records suggest around 20 were sold, some of which had cheaper two-seater replica bodies fitted. Two chassis were built up by Mayfair Coachwork Company, who extended the tail further to

enclose the spare wheel. A further two chassis had MG steel bodies cobbled on to them, with mixed results, and most of the remainder finished up as competition cars or were exported. A few cars suffered disasters during their life and were subsequently rebuilt, sometimes with strange results. The tax rules being what they were, one owner sold the body of his car to the purchaser of a new chassis and then bought himself a new body: in this way the price of both cars was reduced — and the tax likewise. It does not pay for the historian to be too dogmatic about such extreme cases!

The 1100 engine, offside. The belt-driven water pump is prominent (with the belt missing in this case). This car is an Alpine veteran, hence the fuel filter low down on the left, with twin feeds, one to the SU electric pump on the bulkhead and the other to the AC mechanical unit at the base of the distributor. The carburettors fitted here are non-standard.

Turning to the interior of the car, the cockpit was simple and purposeful. The earlier cars had rather a spartan look, as the seating consisted of a common backrest with individual seat cushions, but neat separate seats were introduced in 1937. The seats varied in shape, material and length from the early, short-based 'concrete bun' with coil springs to the later, very comfortable Moseley 'Float on Air' inflatable cushions. All the seats were leather-covered and the same, matching material covered the dashboard on all but the early cars.

Getting into the car, given a little practice, was easy enough and once in the upright seat the driver found the controls well-placed, with the gearlever in the centre of the car, the handbrake to the left of it and the large steering wheel close up. There was limited space around the pedals — the earlier cars had more room with the exposed gearbox and no bulkhead storage. The instrumentation was comprehensive and easily read, with expensive and accurate Jaeger speedometer and chronometric rev-counter usually supplied, together with a vacuum gauge on most later cars. Additional knobs and switches were fitted as required for the various options available to owners, such as telecontrol shock absorbers, spotlights and twin fuel pumps. The early vehicles were equipped with ignition advance-and-retard levers and hand throttles mounted on the steering boss. Later cars with the light Marles steering gear had these controls mounted elsewhere.

As on most sports cars of the time, the weather equipment was a mixture of good, bad and indifferent, but the later cars were reasonably water- and wind-proof with easily-erected protection. The canvas duck hood was mounted on hoops pivoted just behind the seats and it folded neatly inside the line of the body. It could be raised in seconds and located on pegs on the top of the windscreen, then secured by butterfly screws. While early hoods had wraparound quarter panels, these were replaced on the later cars with longer bodies by separate button-on window panels. The sidescreens were steel-framed, slotted into holes set into the door top rails and afforded good protection even with the hood down. Various hinging methods were tried to stop these sidescreens blowing out from the windscreen edge at speed.

The H.R.G. was equipped with a fold-flat windscreen and another 7 to 10mph could be added to the top speed by putting the screen down. The screen pivoted forwards and, unfortunately, presented further sealing problems at the base where a rubber strip was fixed to bridge the gap between the screen and the body panel. This usually worked well, but did have limitations, which could lead to rain water spraying directly onto the occupants — not ideal for impressing the ladies!

On the early cars, the cockpit trimming was minimal, but later, carpet was used to cover the floor, propshaft tunnel, the rear section and the vertical panels in front of the doors. The door panels incorporated map pockets and were trimmed in Rexine or Vyanide. The same material covered the rear compartment sides and back, and the trim panels were all

Engine compartment of a WS series car, with the Singer SM engine installed. The dynamo is driven by the fanbelt and ignition is by coil and distributor. The hydraulic brake fluid reservoir is fitted on the firewall above and behind the steering box.

neatly edged with piping and fixed in position with chromed brass screws in cup washers. The rear compartment floor was hinged to allow access to the rear axle and fuel tank, and some Reall and later bodies were equipped with a tray under this lid, which held the sidescreens. This arrangement was altered in 1949 when the rear vertical panel was hinged down to allow access to a bag behind the fuel tank, which stored the screens.

Two Mayfair bodies were constructed on 1500 chassis. Compared with the standard two-seaters, they are lacking in grace, with square edges much in evidence. The extended tail encloses the spare wheel and a boot space.

By modern standards the interior was narrow and even cramped but, all in all, the H.R.G. was a thoroughly practical sports car. The high quality of the bodies can be seen in the way they have survived, and for something so delicately made of wood and aluminium to last so well, particularly on a flexing, hard-sprung chassis, says a great deal for the skill of the makers.

The Aerodynamic body
The Aerodynamic body was designed to fit on the standard 1500 chassis so that the bare chassis, transmission, brakes and engine were interchangeable. The streamlined front profile required a lower radiator block and a new top water manifold was also designed. Support at the front was provided by a tubular subframe located on the top of the front springs and carried forward over the front axle. Support at the rear was provided by an extension frame bolted to the chassis. The four body mounts at the sides were replaced by longer fittings increasing the body width to 4ft 10in. While all these changes allowed a streamlined vehicle to be produced, they added another 250lb to the car and, in a way, altered the whole character of the H.R.G.

The rounded body panels were made in aluminium and were supported on a framework of square steel tubes. The sectional drawing of the Aerodynamic in Chapter 6 is largely self-explanatory and helps to illustrate the reasons for the basic weaknesses of the car which explain why so few have survived. Flexure of the chassis frame was greatly magnified on the wider-outrigged body panels and components; with heavier items such as the spare wheel, fuel tank and larger doors with wind-up windows to support, fatigue problems were bound to occur. Even so the car did provide more comfort for the occupants and a top speed of up to 10mph higher than the traditionally-styled version. But the extra weight slowed down acceleration and adversely affected roadholding.

On the road
A technical description of the car and its components can only hint at the feel of the machine on the road. The H.R.G. was a purpose-built sporting car and, sitting in the driver's seat, one was immediately aware that the controls fell easily to hand. Steering rake and pedal lengths were adjustable. A pull on the starter brought the engine to life, with a surprisingly low exhaust note from the straight-through Servais silencer and slight noise from the overhead camshaft mechanism of the Singer-based engine.

The engine pulled strongly throughout the usable rev range from 1,500 to 4,500 rpm. In top gear, the engine retained remarkable flexibility despite the high gearing. However, it was the steering and roadholding which were dramatically impressive and these allowed the car to be driven to the limit of its performance under complete control.

Much has been written, largely by those with minimal experience of the marque, on the hard riding and uncomfortable characteristics of the car. The ride *was* firm, but no more so than in other cars with quarter-elliptic suspension and adjustments could easily be made, providing the system was correctly set up and properly maintained. The problems occurred most often due to misinformed adjustments and lack of basic care such as correct lubrication. As far as creature comforts were concerned, the H.R.G. was functional, rather than luxurious, but the fittings were of the highest quality, combining hand craftsmanship with practical good sense.

The car had remarkable 'off road' capabilities, in trials for example, as a result of the weight distribution, and it was a rugged performer on unmade surfaces, such as those of the pre-1952 Alpine rallies.

Each car was supplied with a very comprehensive instruction book and toolkit, enabling the owner to carry out maintenance and repairs with comparative ease supporting the claim that the car was truly the 'Sportsman's Ideal'.

There was admittedly one serious drawback to the H.R.G: the narrow, well-equipped cockpit might be cosy, but the upright bucket seats and the siting of the controls severely restricted amorous activities — but then there is a time and place for everything!

Into production

1937

3

The year 1937 opened with the first international competition appearance of an H.R.G, in the hands of Archie Scott and, of all events, in the Monte Carlo Rally. His car, EPF 97, was in standard trim and Scott started from Umea, in Sweden. Not even the most devoted enthusiast could claim that the H.R.G. was remotely desirable for the journey of some 3,800km to Monte Carlo, in the depths of winter, but Scott not only completed the journey, but drove single-handed. Maurice Gatsonides recalled that the tall, red-moustached Scott and his navigator had wrapped up so thoroughly in fur that from a distance they looked like a couple of bears. It must have been quite an event: the correspondent of *The Times* reported that the chief menaces were stray horses and 'peasants who walked about with their ears covered up because of the intense cold [and] could not hear their horns', which bothered the competitors a lot. After four days, the H.R.G. reached Avignon without penalty and was also unpenalized on the 10km regularity section into Monte Carlo. The strain had undoubtedly taken its toll on Scott and his performance in the acceleration and braking test on the promenade brought him an overall 32nd place and seventh in the $1\frac{1}{2}$-litre class behind Villoresi.

On the home front, Phil Uglow from Callington took a premier award on the Exeter, although Guy Robins, who was in the hunt for a Triple Award, failed gloriously to the detriment of a total of three cars (one left behind with mechanical trouble and one involved in an accident while another one, driven by Curtis, acting as an observer, was also damaged) and the mortification of the factory who ended up with a motley collection of ironmongery on the following Monday morning. Four cars were entered for the JCC Brooklands driving tests in February, with notable performances by Halford and Uglow. This was followed by the only 'works' entry ever made by the company, who nominated a team of three cars driven by Anthony Curtis, Guy Robins and Bill Undery in the RAC Rally. Robins finished second in the 15hp open class, but the team was unplaced in an event notable for snow, ice, rain, sleet and fog. For the Land's End Trial, the weather was replaced as the principal hazard by loads of mud and stones, imported by the organizers. On this occasion, Curtis took a premier award, with third class awards going to Uglow, Robins and Powell.

With the arrival of Anthony Curtis the company embarked on an advertising campaign, featuring the time taken to accelerate from rest to 60mph and brake to a standstill again, the 'Start-Sixty-Stop' figure of 18.4 sec. The guarantee of top speed had been reduced slightly and now merely claimed that the H.R.G. would exceed 85mph. 'Bunny' Dyer, who tested the car for the Junior Car Club Gazette, obtained 87mph with the screen raised. 'On corners', he reported, 'it is startling in that it will scoot round them on a dead level keel, and never yield an inch of side-slip or swing'. A second advertisement added the results of competition success:

1½-litre H.R.G. in standard touring trim made fastest time in Class II, Monte Carlo Rally Test 1937, Brooklands JCC Rally also secured two premier awards. In every competition for which it has been entered, the H.R.G. has proved to be an outstanding performer, frequently beating cars of more than double its capacity. It is outstanding in its liveliness, weighs

Amid the winter snows. The 1½-litre driven by Archie Scott at Umea in northern Sweden for the start of the 1937 Monte Carlo Rally. The tall bear-like figure in the foreground is Scott himself.

only 14cwt and can attain 0-50mph in only 11 seconds — start-60mph-stop in 18²⁄₅ seconds. WHAT IS THREEFOLD PERFORMANCE? It means an H.R.G. owner, for example, may enter his car for a Brooklands event or a reliability trial and still use it as an economical practical means of fast transport, owing to its remarkable versatility. Write for further details — or better still, COME AND DRIVE THIS AMAZING CAR WITHOUT OBLIGATION — Phone or write for an appointment.

Curtis was able to deal with the enquiries which followed at the same time taking on some of the administrative work and releasing Halford to pursue other interests. The order book was now growing and the performance of the cars on the Edinburgh Trial the previous year had much impressed a young man with a Jensen: Peter Clark put his name down for an H.R.G. which was delivered in March, after which the names of Peter Clark and H.R.G. were to become synonymous for more than a decade. Almost all the cars produced went into the hands of competition drivers with the extraordinary exception of one which was only taken out to the river bank on hot days by its owner.

Le Mans, having missed a year in 1936, was back on the calendar and EPF 97 was prepared for Scott, with Ted Halford as the co-driver. There were some 60 entries, of which 49 actually lined up on June 19. The 1½-litre class was contested primarily by British cars and the H.R.G. nearly did not make it at all, having been involved in a contretemps on the way to Le Mans, which required a new front axle and shock absorbers to be flown out. Replacement of same and a spot of radiator soldering put matters to rights, but the H.R.G. was in the pits very early in the race with transmission trouble. Some over-enthusiastic mechanicing had resulted in

A good reason for front-hinged doors. Curtis with the proto-type and a flapping door during a timed test at Hastings on the 1937 RAC Rally.

Ready for the off. The Scott/ Halford 1½-litre EPF 97 in front of the pits awaiting the start of the 1937 Le Mans 24-hour race.

Marcus Chambers attends to the gauze screen of the Scott/ Halford car at Le Mans, 1937. Fred Mead's head is just visible lower down (The Autocar).

Le Mans 1937: the travel-weary crew amid spectators in rather sombre mood at the end of the race. Just visible is the equally travel-weary H.R.G.

44

The Halford Cross Rotary Special on completion. The split front axle is clearly visible, but the standard origins of the chassis, with the lamp bar mountings still in place, can also be seen (T. C. Leaman).

The engine of the Halford Cross Rotary Special, with four Amal carburettors and the Cross cylinder head. The rotary valves were driven off the front of the crankshaft (T. C. Leaman).

the sump being filled twice before the start and, as a result, the clutch was slipping, so surplus oil had to be drawn off and the clutch treated with a fire extinguisher.

Around 8pm, Archie Scott came in with no oil pressure and the motor sounding horrid. The sump was dropped and the fault traced to the bearing feed pipe, which had cracked. A spare was fitted and after an hour and five minutes the car was away again without loss of oil and without breaking the vital Le Mans *plombeur*'s seal. Halford took the car out and promptly drove the next three laps without lights, for which he was in dire danger of disqualification. Thereafter all went well, apart from a weeping fuel tank, which was cured by the entire team chewing gum. By midnight, in heavy rain, the H.R.G. was in second place in its class, behind Skeffington's

45

The Twelve Hour Race at Donington, July 1937. The Scott/Halford H.R.G, on its way to 10th place overall, is here cornering inside Monkhouse's Aston Martin.

Aston Martin, where it remained. Towards the end of the race the results of the oil pipe failure manifested themselves and, on three cylinders at most, the car limped round, making awful noises, in order to qualify for the Biennial Cup, awarded on an index of performance basis over two successive years' races. To achieve this, 164 laps had to be completed and with 163 on the slate and a few minutes to the end of the race, the car was stopped out on the circuit. As the last seconds of the 24 hours ran out, the

Curtis at speed in Coppice Wood during the Donington Twelve Hour Race, 1937.

H.R.G. staggered across the line having averaged 57.2mph, a satisfactory result, but the race was overshadowed by a multiple crash which cost the life of Pat Fairfield.

Halford's interest in racing also manifested itself in another form. The previous year, he had commenced construction of a single-seater racing car incorporating an engine featuring the rotary valve system developed by Mr R.C. Cross. The engine, which was based on the bottom end of a Meadows 4ED, had two separate cylinder blocks, each with a pair of bores. These were fitted on an adaptor plate bolted to the top of the crankcase, but allowing the two blocks to float. Controlled loading was devised for the rotary valves, which were arranged across the aluminium head and driven from the crankshaft by a combination of chains and gears. The valves rotated at half engine speed, being lubricated with oil which was wiped off as they turned. They were designed so that a part of the combustion pressure acted to seal the valve on to the head. The compression ratio was 11:1. Carburation was by four linked Amals without float chambers.

The chassis and running gear were standard H.R.G, the only unusual feature being that the tube of the front axle was split. The body was an offset single-seater made of steel with a high-swept four-branch exhaust manifold emerging from the top of the bonnet on the driver's side. The radiator badge was the H.R.G. trademark shape with the words 'Halford Cross Rotary' superimposed. The car was built up at Oakcroft Road, largely by Halford working in his own time, with the engine installation carried out at Bath by Cross and his draughtsman Coles.

Godfrey had little faith in Cross's ideas and events were to prove him

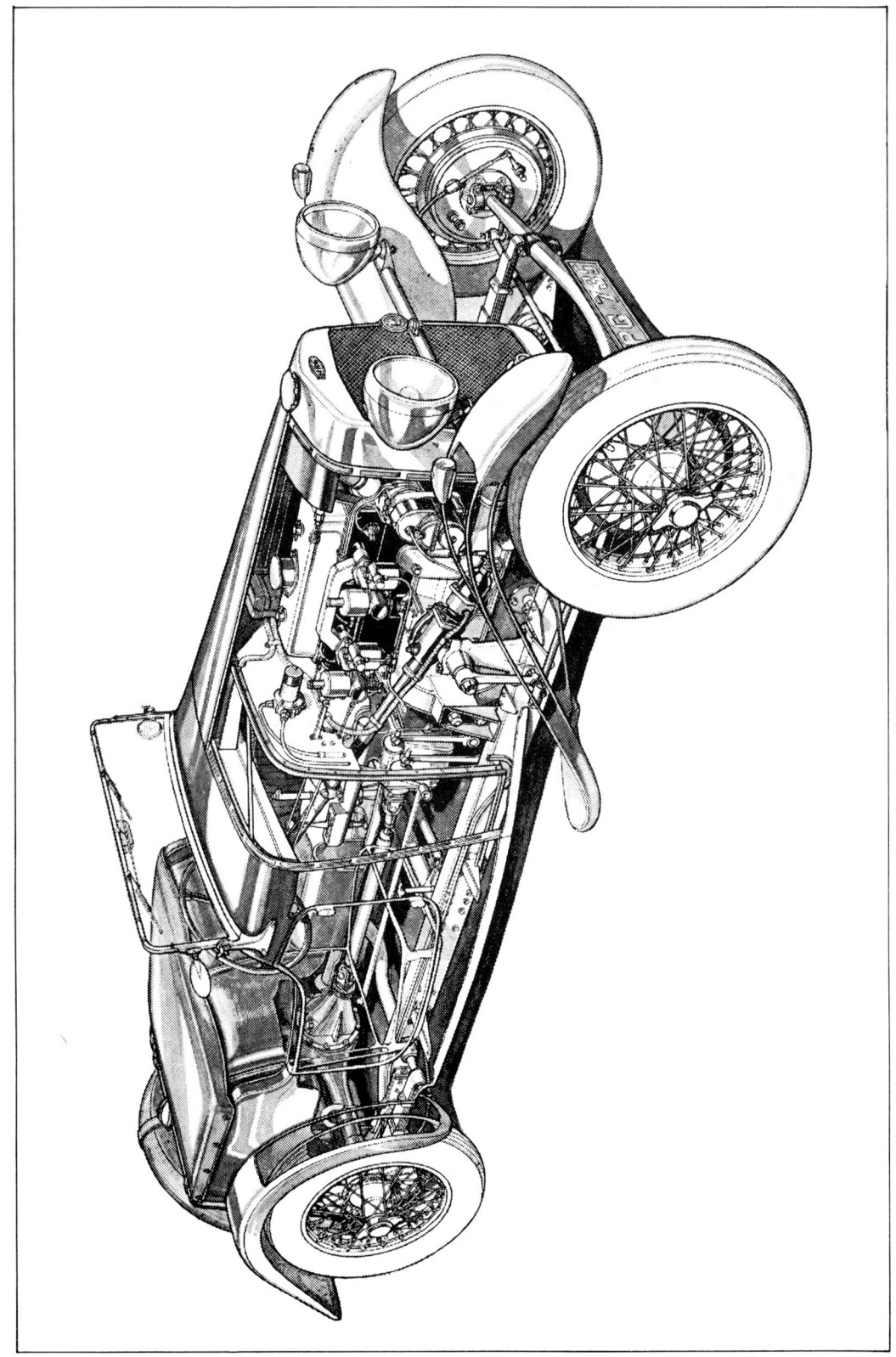

Cutaway drawing showing the layout of the 1½-litre was prepared by Max Millar for The Autocar and used in one of the company's catalogues.

Publicity photo, so redolent of its period, brings together two types of classic British engineering. A 1½-litre 'racing' the Flying Scotsman on a stretch of road in the Midlands (Fox Photos).

right. The car made its appearance at the Backwell Hill Climb, Bristol, in July 1937, in the hands of Joan Richmond, where it managed one ascent in a respectable but not an outstanding time. Halford, driving the prototype 1½-litre, recorded a rather better time. Afterwards, it was taken up to Brooklands for further testing, where, to quote Peter Clark 'it was remarkably fast over the flying inch'. In short, it suffered from the standard headache of rotary valves, seating problems. It was entered for a handicap race on the Outer Circuit and Halford was set to lap at 130mph, no less! When the famous handicapper 'Ebby' Ebblewhite was challenged, he replied that he was not going to be caught out by a car from a factory run by three well-known designers, at which the entry was hurriedly withdrawn. The car was entered in another event, but the valves would not seat and the car did not even have the power to climb the Brooklands banking, and that was that. The Halford Cross Rotary Special was dismantled, the chassis being retained for further use. The Cross head remained at Oakcroft Road until the beginning of the Second World War, when extensions to the concrete driveway required some hardcore. The head being ideal for this purpose, the project was quite literally buried. 'The car was Cross, but not very rotary' (Peter Clark).

The Scott/Halford team was back in action for the Twelve Hour sports car race at Donington on July 24, together with the works demonstrator, EPH 19, in the hands of Curtis, Michael May and motoring writer Alan Hess. In traditional English summer weather, complete with rain and hail, Curtis' team finished fourth overall at 52.65mph, behind Bira's 3.5-litre Delahaye and two Rileys, with Scott and Halford in 10th place, six laps behind Curtis. Their car was heavily handicapped by the lack of a gear selector arm, which had snapped at the base and allowed them to motor in one gear only.

One might have thought that a 'Monte', a Le Mans and a Twelve Hour Race might be enough for one season of motoring, but EPF 97 was out again for the TT race at Donington on September 4, competing in the 1½-litre class with both works-entered and privately-owned Rileys, plus a works 1,122cc Morgan. On this occasion, Scott had as his partner St John Horsfall. The race was run on handicap, with the Rileys and the H.R.G. given two laps and 52 seconds credit, amounting to some 9 miles in 310, with a set speed of 64.2mph. The race was dominated by the 4-litre Talbot Darracqs of Comotti and Lebegue. The H.R.G. started well, being timed at exactly 100mph over the measured quarter-mile, but on the 13th lap Scott came in with a broken oil pipe, which was repaired in three minutes. Once

The red demonstrator on test at Brooklands, 1937. The wiper motor mounted on the top screen rail can be seen: on later cars it was relocated at the base of the screen.

again damage had been done and, after an exciting moment at Melbourne corner, the car began to boil and was withdrawn in the second hour with big-end problems. As far as is known the car never raced again.

Throughout 1937 the 1½-litre remained as the only model in production, but various modifications and improvements were made in the light of experience. From chassis A59 onwards, bucket seats replaced the single rear squabs, and other details were changed. Later in the year, the chassis was widened by 3in, number 66 becoming the first of the W series. The last of the narrow-chassis cars was the company's first export order, delivered to the German driver, Werner Hillegart.

The factory did not exhibit at the Motor Show. Technically the H.R.G. was not eligible, and in any case the cost of exhibiting the car was beyond the resources of the firm. However, an alternative arrangement was made with the co-operation of 'Bunny' Dyer, who ran the Metropolis Garage at Olympia, and a car was displayed there for the benefit of potential customers and the press. During the latter half of the year, the emphasis of activity in the factory began to change, with profitable subcontract general engineering work increasing and the production of cars seeming to be of secondary importance. The year saw the production of just 11 new cars, bringing the total to 17.

Sadly, 1937 ended on a tragic note. One of the new cars had been sold to a university student who, during the Christmas vacation, was involved in an accident. His younger brother, in the passenger seat, was killed and, although the car was not seriously damaged, the factory was instructed to destroy it utterly. Every piece was cut up with a gas torch.

Expansion

1938-1939

4

IT IS RUMOURED THAT A SHORT CHASSIS WILL SOON BE AVAILABLE.

The company was now on a firm footing and the car business was supplemented by machining and subcontract work for nearby engineering establishments, such as Vickers at Weybridge. This created a conflict of interests between car manufacture and other operations, particularly as the general engineering work was profitable. Meanwhile, Halford's position had become rather nebulous and, as he too had become interested in other machinery, particularly gardening equipment, he resigned. His shares in the company were covered by two certificates, one of 124 and the other of 200 shares, and when he left the batch of 124 was purchased equally by David Eadington and Grace Leather. At a later date, the balance of shares were purchased equally by Guy Robins, Richard Churchill, David Eadington and Grace Leather, thus making Robins the largest shareholder and giving David Eadington and Grace Leather a monetary interest in the company, a kind of worker participation. The original batch of shares was bought at a small premium, causing Halford to predict that he would be the only one who would ever make a profit from the company.

With the departure of Halford, Grace Leather was appointed Company Secretary and Curtis assumed a greater degree of responsibility for management. For a short time he was appointed Managing Director, but as he lacked a sound engineering background or experience, the arrangement did not succeed and the management reverted to the earlier dispensation whereby Robins was responsible for engineering, Godfrey for car design and development, and Curtis for sales.

The factory was now developing its second generation of cars. By 1938,

The 1100 proved a successful version of the H.R.G, its shorter wheelbase and lighter engine adding nimble handling to good acceleration. This is a 1939 car in the suitably patrician setting of Bushey Park.

the Meadows 4ED engine was at the end of its production run and a replacement was desirable, particularly if an expansion of car manufacture could be achieved. There was considerable interest in the 1,470cc British Salmson engine, which featured twin overhead camshafts and was manufactured locally, at Raynes Park. However, the choice finally settled on the single-camshaft Singer 12hp engine. In Singer form, the capacity was slightly over 1½ litres, but by installing a shorter-stroke, strengthened crankshaft, made specially by Laystall, a capacity of 1,496cc was achieved. Improvements to almost all the moving parts, and the redesign of the breathing to include a four-branch manifold and twin 1¼in SU carburettors, gave the engine the increased performance required, without loss of reliability. A particular feature of the H.R.G-modified Singer engine was the use of a large-diameter gudgeon pin, which ran straight in the connecting rod without the little-end bush of the original design. The Singer synchromesh gearbox proved quite suitable in standard form, although minor improvements to the provisions for lubrication were carried out.

To test the new engine, GPE 607, the latest factory demonstration car (called the 'green demonstrator' to distinguish it from the earlier 'red demonstrator' EPH 19) had its Meadows engine extracted and the Singer-based unit substituted. The engine was thoroughly tested and a few were installed, but before full production could get under way the project was overtaken by events of vastly greater magnitude on the international scene.

In terms of numbers, the second 1938 development, announced at the works dinner, was more immediately successful. From the start, the idea of building an 1,100cc version of the car had been in Godfrey's mind, and the Singer 9hp engine proved to be most suitable. As described in Chapter 2, the 1100 was really a short-chassis version of the 1½-litre car and its initial acceleration, using the 4.55:1 rear axle, was not far short of the larger model's, with a 0-30mph figure of 4.8 seconds. Its overall maximum speed was around 80mph. At first, the engine was installed with a single exhaust manifold, but was soon modified to the more normal four-branch arrangement. Twin 1⅛in SU carburettors supplied the mixture. Although not as powerful as the larger-engined cars, the 1100 could still give a good account of itself in competitive events, largely due to its lighter engine and improved handling. It weighed in at 1,510lb, 60lb lighter than the 1½-litre, and its price of £289 compared well with the 1½-litre, which by now sold at £424 12s 6d. A second spare wheel cost a further £7 10s 0d, a 'Brooklands' bonnet strap £1 7s 6d and colours other than the standard blue, black, green or red, all with black wheels, cost an extra £2 10s 0d.

The 1100 bodies, built by Reall, were the first to accommodate the petrol tank within the body. Whereas the rear of the Croft bodies fell vertically,

The Triumph-engined coupe-bodied H.R.G. on its first appearance, at Brooklands in August, 1938 (The Motor).

Three-quarter rear view of the coupe. The attempt to be in vogue — MG had offered a similar Airline body on the PB a couple of years earlier — was not a great success, and it remained a one-off experiment.

the 1100 and subsequently the 1500 bodies were angled so that the spare wheel fitted snugly against the rear panel. The petrol filler cap was mounted first on the nearside rear corner, then moved to the rear panel itself, alongside the spare wheel. A total of seven 1100s were produced in 1938-39.

Following the dismemberment of the Halford Cross Rotary Special, the chassis was rebuilt in wide form as Halford's last project, constructed during the winter of 1937-38. In this case, a Triumph 1,600cc engine was installed and a most elegant white, fixed-head coupe body fitted. The design, which was more or less standard H.R.G. up to the windscreen line, featured a flowing tail with a semi-recessed spare wheel, two large doors and sliding glass windows. The windscreen could be opened and a sunroof was fitted. The front wings were extended rearwards to runningboards, joined to the rear wings which appeared to flare upwards, giving a high rear gound clearance. Other features included trafficators and a walnut

Profile of the Le Mans model H.R.G. prepared to the order of Archie Scott for Le Mans 1938 though not in the end driven there. The factory offered replicas but there were no takers.

54

dashboard. The car was catalogued at £475. If looks alone could ensure success the coupe would have been a winner, but following its introduction in the Brooklands paddock in the summer, it proved to be somewhat of an embarrassment. The body did not flex sympathetically with the chassis and consequently the doors had their own ideas on when to open. It never got as far as a road test and was rapidly christened the 'White Elephant'. The car hung around for some time and was finally disposed of in a deal which involved the trade-in of a Riley of uncertain quality: part-exchanges were not indulged in thereafter!

Also during the 1937-38 winter, chassis W73 was built up to the order of Archie Scott, the target being Le Mans, with the specific intention of winning the Biennial Cup for which he had (just) qualified the previous year. It was by no means impossible — in 1937 the cup had been won in an Aston Martin by Mort Morris-Goodall, who had finished in 11th place only. As it so happened, Scott got married instead and the entry lapsed, but the car was completed for him and announced as the 'Le Mans' model, a semi-racing two-seater. The Meadows engine was fully tuned, with raised compression, and every nut on the car was split-pinned or wired. Various racing additions were fitted, including a larger petrol tank with twin filler caps, twin fuel-feed lines, a lap scorer on the dashboard, a gauze windscreen and aero screens, two bonnet straps and Le Mans sealing tags. The rear of the body was redesigned and built by Crofts, with a streamlined, pointed tail covering the tank and twin spares mounted

Detail of the Le Mans model. Inside the tail, left, the twin spare wheels were mounted horizontally on the rear spring bearer tube. Headlamps protected by stoneguards and cycle-type wings gave the car a distinctively purposeful and sporting look, right.

Bill Boddy at the wheel of DPA 233, the prototype H.R.G, taking part in the speed trials at Lewes in Sussex.

horizontally. Lightweight cycle mudguards were fitted all round and the total weight was 1,610lb. The Le Mans model was offered at £495, with an 1,100cc version optional at £365. The option was never taken up and, like the coupe, total production was one.

By now H.R.Gs were out in force and were serious competition contenders. 1938 opened with a clutch of six premier awards on the Exeter trial, led by Phil Uglow with his new 1½-litre. Once again, Guy Robins took second place in class in the RAC Rally, putting up best performance in class in the special tests at Blackpool. By the spring, there was a regular circus of drivers — Robins and Curtis with the works cars, the Perkins brothers, West with Uglow's old car, Baillie Hill the H.R.G. apprentice, Ken Farley, and Elsie Redfern — to name a few. At the Lewes speed trials in May, a special class for H.R.Gs was run, with John Eason Gibson, Robins' wife Dora, and Curtis' wife Nancy, all joining in the fun. Another well-known figure who drove the prototype, DPA 233, at Lewes was a young journalist from *Motor Sport*, William Boddy.

'Ant' Curtis, as Secretary of the Light Car Club, was interested in organizing several events at Brooklands and, in the teeth of disapproval from Godfrey, he arranged for GPE 607 to be loaned to Prince Birabongse.

Bira was by now a household name and there was even a suggestion that the company might pay him for what might be valuable publicity. This was too much for Godfrey, who pointed out that he could find plenty of people who would drive — and probably blow up — one of his cars and might even pay for the privilege. Nonetheless Curtis carried the day and when arrangements were made for Bira and his cousin Prince Chula to visit the factory one afternoon, it was felt that some effort should be made to tidy up both office and workshop. Curtis and Grace Leather cleared the desks by gathering up papers, correspondence and the like, putting it all in a small metal cupboard and pushing the door shut. To their utter surprise and confusion, Price Chula opened the door of the cupboard to be met by an avalanche of the contents. It was hurriedly explained that it was an old Siamese custom to open cupboard doors or drawers of your host to show that you believed there was nothing to hide, but both the members of staff concerned were highly sceptical of the explanation and never again made any effort to be other than normal — untidy, but reasonably efficient. Bira duly drove the car in the Brooklands Whit Monday meeting, finishing third in the Star Trophy sports car handicap.

In July, the Light Car Club promoted a three-hour sports car race for catalogue sports cars, which was not well-supported. However, the field included a Delahaye, a gaggle of Frazer-Nash-BMWs and representatives

Bira lifts the inside front wheel as he makes up time after the replacement of the gearlever: Brooklands Production Sports Car Race, 1938 (Klemantaski).

from Morgan, SS, Railton, Allard, Hotchkiss and Alvis, plus Bira as the sole 1½-litre class entry with the H.R.G. he had driven at Whitsun, its foot pedals fully extended to suit his short stature.

Bira made a good start, which included all drivers having to lower their hoods, but by the 20th lap he was in the pits with a gearbox selector problem. This was unfortunate for Bira, but even more so for Harold Powell, whose car was parked nearby in the paddock. It was immediately raided for spares and Bira rejoined the race. At the end of the race, the rear tyres were changed in the smartish time of 40 seconds and the car ran home tenth overall, a rather hollow class winner.

The green demonstrator was also loaned to R. de Yarburgh-Bateson, an architect and, as 'Arthur', a well-known motoring cartoonist, for the Paris-Nice Trial. For this, the pedals were re-adjusted, Arthur being as tall as Bira was short. The car finished first in the class, with best performance in class on the La Turbie hill-climb.

Although Archie Scott had scratched from Le Mans, Peter Clark and Marcus Chambers, forming 'L'Ecurie du Lapin Blanc', had also entered for the event, using Peter's 1½-litre, DYV 221. The British contingent was rather thin on the ground, the only larger British car than Peter's being the Hitchins/Morris-Goodall 2-litre Aston Martin. The race itself was one in which retirements played a significant part and the Clark/Chambers car rose steadily from 28th place at the end of 6 hours to 15th at half-distance and 10th at 18 hours. In the last period of the race the leading Alfa Romeo of Sommer/Biondetti and the Aston in ninth place both retired, but the H.R.G. began to weaken and eventually progressed on less than its accustomed four cylinders, allowing Savoye's Singer and a Simca-Fiat to

GPE 607 again: R. de Yarburgh-Bateson with the green demonstrator in the Paris-Nice Trial, 1938, on the way to a class win (Dognibene).

pass. It finally finished, still in 10th place, at an average speed of 59.63mph, to take second place in the class behind the Lohr/Von Guilleaume Adler. Peter wrote up the story of the event in a letter to *Motor Sport.* Modestly, he refers to removing 'a few pieces' to enable the car to finish — at least one of them was a connecting rod!

Le Mans, as far as I am concerned, wrote Peter Clark, *really started on February 28, after the Colmore trial. Marcus Chambers, who was to prepare the car for racing, had been nagging me since November about my continuing to 'break it up', as he called it.*

Well, he took it all to pieces, and considering it had hardly missed a trial since the previous June, there were not many things broken. He re-assembled the chassis first, lock-nutting everything. Then he started on the engine, and it is only fair to say that most of the things he decided to do were in the nature of hoped-for improvements, rather than necessary repairs; all the bearings and so on were perfect after 16,000 miles of hard competition work. The car ran at the March Brooklands meeting and at a Donington Club event with hardly any coachwork on at all and we satisfied ourselves that, subject to a final overhaul, the performance was satisfactory. In the matter of coachwork, I wanted a tail and an undershield in the hope that this would give a 'cruising maximum' of 80 to 85mph on a smaller throttle

The tail of DYV 221 as finally constructed, a foot or so shorter than the original. On the dashboard can be seen part of the revised electrical system, with individually-switched circuits for each item.

59

Finishers at Le Mans, 1938. DYV 221 with Chambers (at the wheel) and Clark, and the Miss Fawcett/G. White 1,098cc Morgan, respectively first and second British cars home, alongside the streamlined 1,679cc Adler of Orssich and Sauerwein which won the Rudge Whitworth Biennial Cup.

opening than would otherwise be the case; a great asset in a long race. On the other hand, I did not want to sacrifice the excellent luggage space of the standard H.R.G. body in view of the necessity of carrying all spares and tools on the car at Le Mans. Our first effort in this direction appeared at the Easter Brooklands meeting, but during motoring backwards a great deal during practice, and nearly doing so once during the race, I decided our tail was too long and had about a foot sawn off. The final result was seen at Shelsey.

I was not entirely satisfied with my time at Shelsey, for although I carried full Le Mans equipment and the special gears were far too high, I felt that all our careful tuning should have enabled me at least to equal my time last year, stripped but with a perfectly standard engine. We therefore decided, whilst not competing in the Brooklands Whitsun meeting, to do a spot of practising to 'see if anything fell off'. Something did. Bystanders said it was one of the most complete auto-dismantlements they had seen for ages. There we were, Saturday before Whitsun Bank Holiday, seven days before shipping abroad, and a good deal of our engine strewn along the Railway Straight. Things certainly looked black, for few engineering firms would be open even on Tuesday, so that Wednesday or Thursday was the earliest we could hope for parts to begin rebuilding the engine, and we already had a full programme of last minute 'sundries'.

Then I remembered that Ken Farley, the well-known trials H.R.G. exponent, was about to get married, and he might not be using his H.R.G. on his honeymoon. I rang him up and he very sportingly offered his engine. On Whit Monday, ably assisted by one of the directors of Bochaton Motors (who look after Ken's car), we took the two engines to pieces and rebuilt a 'new' one from selected parts of both. As dawn broke on Tuesday, I pressed the starter button and it worked.

So we set off on the appointed day, slept soundly on the non-upholstered shelves on the boat, and in due course reached Le Mans; a journey memorable, perhaps, for our Chef d'Equipe's *request to a garage near Dieppe, on finding his Lancia's tyres a little soft for the unwonted load of spares and tools. Translated literally, he asked them to 'whistle a bit in the wheels'. Eventually came the great day. The car had run well in practice, but our hotch-potch engine was naturally rather an unknown quantity, and we decided to limit ourselves to a maximum of 3,800rpm. This gave us less than 80mph in top, but by using the wonderful cornering and brakes of the H.R.G. to the full, we could lap at about 64mph. We had heard a lot about the dire effects of the heat and/or the fuel on valves and as a result rather overdid the rich mixture stunt; I oiled a plug after about an hour and again an hour later. This was an annoying waste of time but was an opportunity to lash up one of the headlights which had broken adrift, as well as weakening the mixture.*

After that all went well for about 130 laps; we made up the time lost by those two early pit stops and were running about 5mph ahead of qualifying speed. Two hours before the end a derangement in the valve gear caused an involuntary stop, but after removing a few pieces the car was able to proceed and was actually lapping at about 48mph on two (and occasionally three) cylinders. On the following day, we broached our chestful of spares (unused during the race) and did what was necessary to the engine. Incidentally, on our return to England, it was clapped straight back into Ken Farley's car without further attention for him to run in the JCC show at Brooklands, so the 'derangement' was not too serious. Having ascertained during the race that the French idea of a 'properly constructed' silencer is none other than a straight-through pipe, we childishly decided to construct one for the return journey, and therefore hied us to a steam-roller breakers as being a likely purveyor of a suitable sewer. The requisite pipe, in metric figures, was a rather uneven and unusual size but our friend armed with an oxy-acetylene cutter on a mountain of metal, scorned callipers and selected a pipe by eye. It was with misgivings that we brought it back (eight miles) but surprisingly enough, it fitted perfectly.

61

Curtis at Bude with the 1100 during the 1939 MCC Land's End Trial in which he gained a premier award. The full-depth transparent sidescreen was later replaced by one with the more usual flap across the lower section.

Incidentally, we found the standard of welding and so on and the speed with which one can get special bits made up in France quite amazing.

Thus ended the best holiday of my life, and although nine people spent the whole of their spare time for six months talking, thinking, dreaming and planning nothing else, it was only a holiday and a very amateur little effort compared with the wonderfully organized (and financed) Continental entries. More is the pity. And anyone who says 'You can do Le Mans on a hundred quid' is talking through a portion of his anatomy intended by nature for quite another purpose.

Peter having injured himself in a hill-climbing accident in August, DYV

Curtis with the prototype 1100 again, negotiating a special test on Madeira Drive, Brighton, during the 1939 RAC Rally (Klemantaski).

Le Mans 1939: Peter Clark accelerates away from the start to begin a trouble-free run to 14th place overall and the 1½-litre class win.

Clark's 1½-litre being followed through the Esses by a Delahaye and an Adler in the early stages of the 1939 Le Mans race.

221 was driven in the TT at Donington by Marcus Chambers, with a second entry from Werner Hillegart. The 1½-litre cars were set to lap at 65.8mph, which proved too much and Chambers' H.R.G. finished 18th overall and 6th in class, Hillegart managing 4th in class and 16th overall at an average of 59.69mph.

A visitor to the factory at this time was Godfrey's old associate Stuart Proctor, who had developed a small aircraft engine which needed to be tested. Godfrey, as owner of the Oakcroft Road site, gave Proctor permission to erect a facility at the end of the works on which the engine could be run for the requisite number of hours and the tests lasting at least eight hours a day were carried out to the complete satisfaction of the designer, but not to the company, who were blamed for the monotonous noise by residents nearly half a mile away. Fortunately, the locals did not seem to be worried and as the local authority had specified that occupiers on the industrial estate could make any noise appertaining to their business, the matter was taken no further. The engine passed its proving trials, but Proctor was never able to capitalize on it as the firms who might have been interested were involved in tooling up for war work. The engine

W.P. Uglow and Ashley Cleave achieved many successes in trials, races and speed events with DRL 540, both with the original Meadows engine and later with a Riley 1½-litre power unit. The pioneering spirit is evident in this prewar West Country trial scene.

Opposite: Marcus Chambers brings the 1½-litre into the pits, Le Mans 1939. On each side of the bonnet top just behind the radiator is the white rabbit motif of L'Ecurie du Lapin Blanc.

remained at the factory and was only disposed of at the closure.

The early months of 1939 saw the 'circus' reinforced by the 1½-litres of Ken Delingpole and Mike Lawson, plus Curtis with the prototype 1100, HPF 134. There were four premier awards on the Exeter and two on the Land's End, one going to Curtis, proving that the 1100 was a potent trials performer. Lawson also had a very good run in the RAC Rally, but an outright win eluded the marque.

Peter Clark and Marcus Chambers were back at Le Mans in June. Archie Scott had also had an entry, but again withdrew. The entry list was notable for the appearance of the new Lagondas, one in the hands of Peter Mitchell-Thompson, Lord Selsdon. This time, the H.R.G. ran faultlessly and it worked steadily up the field, finishing in 14th place at an average speed of 67.307mph to win the 1½-litre class.

Clark could see clearly that the H.R.G. was unlikely to go any quicker and it would be only a matter of time before the all-enveloping aerodynamically-designed cars already being built on the Continent would dominate sports-car racing. His opinions were shared at the factory and already the directors were looking forward into the 1940s. Despite the international crisis which rumbled on, a plan of campaign for expansion and modernization was drawn up, based on the use of easily-available Singer components. Stage One was to be the settling-in period during which production would be increased to around 150 cars, both 1100s and 1500s.

During this time a new prototype was to be built up and tested. The principal features were to be as follows:

Engine. The Singer bottom end would be used, but with an aluminium head, possibly of new design, with water-cooled bronze valve guides. Dural rods, running directly on the crankshaft, would be made and a full-flow oil filter and large electron sump fitted. Low-boost supercharging would be considered.

Gearbox. Suitable close-ratio gears would be found.

Chassis. Dural would replace mild steel, including bolts. Leg room would be increased and the body widened. The chassis was to be redesigned to accommodate an 1,100cc, 1,500cc or 2-litre engine.

Rear Axle. A lighter casing would be designed, with improved hub mountings.

Front Axle. Independent front suspension to be fitted.

Brakes. Twin-leading-shoe layout in front, single at the rear, with magnesium brake shoes and hydraulic operation.

Body. All-enveloping, fully streamlined, similar to the sports-racing BMWs, with a drophead coupe and/or closed model. The various bodies, plus the existing two-seater to be interchangeable on the chassis.

A production run of some 200 of these cars was forecast and it was hoped that economies in scale of production would compensate for the increased cost of lighter materials. Peter Clark was consulted on the competition side and useful advice on the bodywork was provided by Yarburgh-Bateson. In fact, the whole project was starting to roll regardless of the rapidly deteriorating political situation. It was business as usual up to the last moment and Werner Hillegart was entered for the TT scheduled to be held at Donington on September 2, 1939. He decided to stay at home, the race was cancelled and on the following day the country was at war.

Hostilities

5

1939-1945

Having already acquired a background of general engineering work prior to 1939, the company benefited from the stepping up of the armaments programme. Not only did the contracts from Vickers increase, but the company became acceptable to other aircraft manufacturers, such as Bristol and Armstrong Whitworth, and in due course was able to tender and obtain contracts direct with the relevant ministries. For the first two years of the war some time was spent completing partly finished car parts and storing the various components, jigs and patterns in the expectation of future use. The problem of storage was solved by constructing a floor between the rafters and the roof of the main building.

Several H.R.Gs were in use on essential war work and these were serviced up to 1942, after which the company was fully engaged on various types of armament work. During the early stages of the war, the factory issued advice to owners on improving petrol economy. The compression ratio on the Meadows engine could be lowered to 6:1, thus giving improved fuel consumption, by means of using a second head gasket or by slipping $\frac{3}{32}$in spacers between the cylinder block and the crankcase. Owners of 1100s were recommended to fit weaker carburettor needles.

Wartime production: a 'Locator' direction-finder for aircraft detection in use on a factory roof.

Wartime plans: the mock-up of the streamliner body as originally proposed. The height of the body behind the seating area is much lower here than in the form that eventually reached production.

The factory, which was on the same estate as Siebe Gorman, Powered Mountings, Nash & Thompson and Parnell Aircraft, was in a security zone and was camouflaged as well as being protected by barbed wire and the Home Guard, all rather different from the free-and-easy prewar years. As with many other engineering companies, the problem of staff being called up created many difficulties, with trained men leaving to be replaced, in due course, by men of mediocre ability, and these then replaced by even less competent people. The factory took on many more hands to deal with the many items they were now called on to produce, and at one time there were 80 employees on the payroll, including a night shift. In case of air attack, an air-raid shelter was constructed behind the building: unfortunately it tended to flood and, as the pressure of production steadily increased, so it became used less and less.

Guy Robins was a Flying Officer in the RAFVR at the outbreak of war,

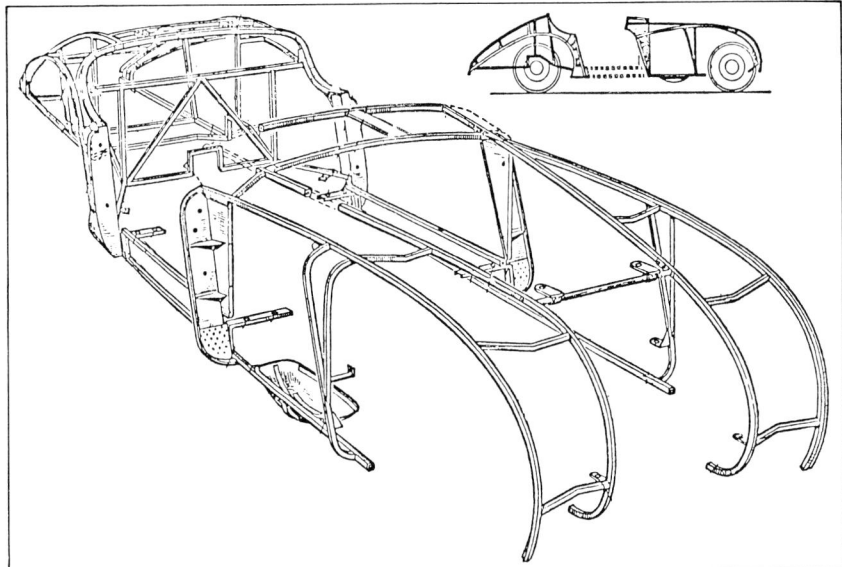

but in view of his occupation his call-up was deferred and he remained at the factory for the entire wartime period. Godfrey was over the age for active service, but Curtis stayed at Oakcroft Road for only a short while before joining the Grand Union Canal Company in an executive capacity.

The range of items produced at Oakcroft Road was extremely diverse. A new aperture gunsight was produced after Dunkirk in order to improve the accuracy of a wide range of equipment, including Lewis and Bofors guns, Hispano cannons and any other weapons that could be pressed into service. Thousand of handles for winching bombs into the bays of Wellington bombers were fabricated, as were the rolls for providing the curved sections of Barnes Wallis' fuselage design for that aircraft. Later on, miniature aerials were constructed for use by the paratroop forces. Designed for communications with aircraft or tanks, they were at one time in such demand that when each batch of three or four were completed a despatch rider came and collected them.

Another unusual production item was the 'Locator', which was a steel, saucer-shaped, early-warning directional indicator. This could provide information on the precise path of approaching enemy aircraft, which enabled key operations to be continued until the very last moment in the case of a general alert. The equipment was designed by John C. Gilbert, a lecturer at the Northern Polytechnic, who also owned an H.R.G. and later became better known as the presenter of a TV inventor's programme. Mobile mountings for industrial and medical X-ray equipment were manufactured. Many of these items required careful inspection arrangements as well as highly detailed costing procedures, both of which were put to good use in later years. Likewise, such a diversity of materials and components called for improved office and stores systems and these, too, were valuable acquisitions.

As the war drew to a close, the company began to prepare itself for the resumption of car manufacture. The parts and drawings were brought out, but it was clear that a different style of production would be necessary. One lesson learned from wartime production was that small batches were not as economic as long runs, and it followed that there would need to be an increase in finance to enable the company to carry larger stocks. Another conclusion reached was that sales would need specialized and expert handling. These and other similar matters were under discussion, as witnessed by a list of items for consideration at a board meeting at the end of 1944, including 'Postwar car modifications of a new design'. There was also the possibility of a new 'Small car engine' and a fascinating and cryptic item covering 'B & M fixtures for secret machine'.

The war years had, of course, brought about a cessation of the developments planned in 1939. A wooden mock-up of a streamlined body had been constructed for fitting on a standard chassis and, although the design concept was largely that of Robins, both Clark and Yarburgh-Bateson had spent some time looking for ideas and making proposals. Yarburgh-Bateson had sketched the design of a body for fitting to his AC which was remarkably similar to the new streamliner and *The Motor* had printed a 'faked' photograph of Clark's 1940 racing design, complete with action background. Clark, however, had second thoughts, which were published in a letter to *The Motor*.

Le Mans is quite likely to be the first notable event in the postwar racing calendar, he wrote. *Let us consider the car. It must be capable of putting up a (calculated) winning performance without having to exceed safe cruising rpm. The car must be restful and inspiring to conduct; I can rule out altogether cars which progress in a series of bounds and swerves..... What sort of car will meet these straightforward requirements? I do not intend at this stage to concern myself with engine or structural details,*

The prototype Aerodynamic as first completed. Headlights have yet to be fitted and there is much need of detail refinement.

70

beyond saying that to win the 1½-litre class and the Rudge Whitworth Cup our car must be capable of a sustained 130mph. This could be forthcoming from an 1,100cc unit with moderate boost, subject to lightweight and efficient streamlining. I am going to sit upright; I am going to see where I am going, and I am probably going to achieve these objects by some form of forward control..... Some readers may remember the details published about my 1940 H.R.G. which got as far as construction of the chassis, blueprints of the body and a small model of the body and a small model of the whole. Modifying the seating position of my prewar H.R.G. to conform with the hypothetical new body convinced me that the car would have been a pig to drive..... The seat of my forward-control machine will be bench type with a wide pull-down central arm. Should we have independent front suspension? I don't care a hoot as long as we understeer. Some of the best cars I have ever handled had normal suspensions, some of the worst had IFS..... I demand a close-ratio crash gearbox. Brakes must be adjustable in motion from the driving seat. I shall be happy with 4.50 x 16 front and 5.00 x 17 rear tyres, with knock-on hubs..... Fuel tank or tanks admidships, so that the varying load will not affect roadholding, with separate pipelines on opposite sides of the chassis. Spare wheels in the tail aft and batteries inside the false bonnet in front. Headlamps set very low, with a foglamp between them and all three enclosed by a single panel of glass. Instruments will include an oil-level gauge, a readily accessible and positive reserve oil tap and separate switches for every electrical item. Fuses to be accessible for changing in motion. There will be no choke, hand

Three-quarter rear view of the prototype Aerodynamic. The flowing lines of the mock-up somehow did not survive the panel-beating stage and the car needed considerable improvement before it reached production, for example by redesigning the door hinge arrangement.

throttle or ignition controls as I have been fated by any and all of them coming adrift..... So, come along gentlemen. You build it and I will drive it. Not only will I win races for you with the thing, I will also buy one for everyday family use. It was all good fighting talk and such dreams kept the enthusiast going during the hostilities.

Yarburgh-Bateson came up with several ingenious ideas for the bodywork details, producing a design for pop-up headlamps (cable-operated) and a quick-acting jack. He even suggested the fitting of a Pitot tube feeding an air speed indicator on the dashboard. In practice, the prototype body, when it finally appeared, contained none of these exotic items, nor sadly the very stylish art-deco radiator grille with inbuilt headlamps that was originally proposed. More fundamentally, the body was designed to be fitted to the existing chassis, the independently-suspended proposal of 1939 having failed to materialize.

The new body was constructed on a skeleton of square steel tubes which was designed in two separate sections, fore and aft. These were joined only by two tubes acting as lower rails behind the door-line. The whole frame was located on the chassis and subframes at 12 points. The tube itself had well-radiused edges, over which the aluminium panels were wrapped and secured with screws. In an attempt to reduce squeaks, anti-chafing strips were placed between the skin and the frame.

But before any of these or other plans could be implemented, there were more practical matters to be resolved. Licences for the supply of materials had to be sought and there were difficulties in obtaining many items that had been produced before the war. Suppliers were now talking about minimum quantities and some were not even ready to resume peacetime manufacture. Electricity to run the factory was subject to power cuts, a problem solved by Robins who, at Godfrey's suggestion, harnessed a 1500 engine to provide power for the machine shop. This was possible as the shop was equipped with belt-driven machines, but it did not overcome the snag that petrol was very strictly rationed. Eventually, a diesel generator was obtained: this provided the required power, but nearly vibrated the factory out of existence before the surrounding concrete slab was cut away from the main floor, after which it remained in use until the electricity supply became more reliable.

At this point, Robins put forward the view that the company should move to more suitable premises. He felt that the existing buildings were inadequate in size, and costly both to heat and to maintain. He followed up the proposal by locating a unit he considered suitable, a wartime food storage building known as a Buffer Depot. This was sited at Betchworth, Surrey, some miles from Tolworth and was consequently not considered suitable by the other directors, since all the key personnel walked or bicycled to Oakcroft Road from the Tolworth and Kingston areas. Instead, the company decided to purchase a temporary building from the nearby Fox & Nicholl garage and erect it on the land at the rear of the factory. This was a timber-framed building, covered with felt and corrugated asbestos, which was used as an engine and fitting shop. Although termed portable and temporary it remained in position for the next 20 years. It was, however, a disappointment to Robins that the opportunity to remove some of the difficulties that had grown up during the first 10 years of the company had been lost.

Austerity

1945-1947

With the coming of peace in 1945, the company realized that it was now faced with the necessity to resolve three major problems. Firstly, on the basis of the prototype streamlined car, the possibility of sales in quite substantial numbers looked good. However, the question of the supply of a sufficient quantity of bodies was unresolved, particularly as the limited number of specialist coachbuilders were now in great demand and were generally over-committed. Secondly, both Halford and Curtis having departed, there was no sales force in the company. Robins, in particular, believed that sales should be undertaken by an independent organization, quite separate from the factory, to handle customers' requirements in the normal manner of the motor trade. Thirdly, in order to produce an increasing number of cars, the company's financial structure needed strengthening and plans were drawn up to try and obtain extra funding. It was thought that whoever might put up extra capital might also take an active managerial role in the company.

While attending to these urgent and weighty matters, the management also had to get the day-to-day running of the factory back on a more normal, peacetime footing. Many of the original employees had been demobilized and, as the war contracts finished, the workforce was reduced and the company reverted to its old activities, combining car production with general engineering.

The matter of the bodies was resolved through Fox & Nicholl, whose garage, a short way up the Kingston Bypass, was associated with Lagondas and Talbots before the war. The manager found he now had the space, capacity and labour available to undertake sheet metalwork and, although the firm were not coachbuilders, it was arranged that Fox & Nicholl should construct the bodies for the new streamliner. An order for 100 was placed

at the cost of around £250 each. Meanwhile, the standard two-seater bodies would continue to be built by Reall.

The sales problem was tackled through an old Brooklands friend of Godfrey, Charles Follett, who ran a successful motor business in Berkeley Street, London W1. At a time when anything new on four wheels had an immediate sale, Follett was happy to act as concessionaire for H.R.G. in addition to his Rolls-Royce, Bentley and Lea-Francis distributorships. Follett's customers were of a very different type to the original, prewar factory customers, but the advanced looks of the streamlined car, which was now christened the Aerodynamic, were likely to appeal to his clientele.

Follett in his turn was able to assist from the financial angle and introduced Lord Selsdon (Peter Mitchell-Thompson of prewar Frazer-Nash and Lagonda fame), and T.A.S.O. Mathieson. Selsdon was already known to Godfrey and Robins, while Mathieson was also connected with motor sport, being a member of the RAC Competitions Committee. In 1946, the company's capital was restructured and the original debenture redeemed. Selsdon and Mathieson provided extra funds, and Selsdon, who now had a controlling shareholding, became Chairman. In fact, the company ended up with only an extra £3,000 at its disposal, which was rather less than originally envisaged. David Eadington relinquished the board position he had held during the war years, but Mathieson did not join immediately as his place on the RAC Competitions Committee prevented him from taking a direct commercial involvement.

This move initially appeared to resolve the matter of extra managerial

expertise. Although not an executive director, Selsdon was keen to promote the company's products and was instrumental in arranging a US outlet through Hoffman Motors in New York, who sold three Aerodynamics. A total of nine cars were shipped to South America, where most, if not all, survive. Other cars were taken to motor shows in Prague and Brussels. The Swedish agents Alpen, Gunderson AB sold five, one of which started a young man named Joachim Bonnier on his road to racing fame. Gosta Alpen himself had a number of successes with his 1500 in racing and the cars also performed well on the rough Scandinavian rally courses and in ice racing. Other cars were exported to Africa and to Australia.

At one stage, preliminary discussions were held to determine whether it might be possible to attack the US market more effectively by forming a combined sales outlet with Aston Martin and possibly Allard, but the idea came to nothing.

On the home front, the difficulties of supply and delivery continued to create problems for the company, while the Aerodynamic bodies were a problem in their own right. These would have been far more suited to an independently-suspended, rigid chassis and, outrigged as they were on the flexible standard chassis, they began to rattle and come apart. The trouble was mostly inherent in the design, but could have been eased somewhat by the use of better fixings on the panels. Unlike changes within the factory, it was difficult to get Fox & Nicholl to make modifications as they became necessary. On the sales side, the Follett organization wanted to sell cars rather than deal with numerous detail complaints from their clients, who

The machine shop at Oakcroft Road, well equipped for general engineering in addition to providing the vital force for car production.

tended to think that a sports car was just the same as anything else on the road, but with good looks, and should not require any special attention. The net result was that, far from distancing themselves from the customers, the factory staff found themselves becoming more involved than ever.

No matter how grim the situation was — and the winter of 1946-47 was grimmer than most — there were the occasional lighter moments. One new owner of an Aerodynamic was an art connoisseur whose car was left at the

No substitute for experience. Lord Selsdon, who was to play an important part in the restructuring of the company, is introduced to the prototype Aerodynamic, still in its original form, by Fred Mead.

factory for minor electrical adjustments. On his return the same evening he found the car waiting on the forecourt, so he stepped from his chauffeur-driven limousine and stowed an oil painting in the boot of the H.R.G. The engine was started and as he prepared to move off he switched on the lights, but unfortunately these had somehow been wired to the horns. Enraged, he leapt from the sonorous car, hurled his bowler hat away in fury and tossed into the limousine the painting followed by the umbrella, the latter impaling the former. At this point, the chauffeur was summoned to retrieve the hat, something which was much easier said than done, as it had come to rest on the top of the coke pile outside the office! The car was collected later, but the owner was never seen again.

Engines were still a matter of concern as it was clear that the Singer block had reached the limit of its reliable power output. Investigations were made into the possible use of Riley engines, and discussions were held at Rovers with the Wilks brothers, but both units were rejected as not powerful enough and too heavy, a critical factor in the roadholding balance of the standard chassis. A Jowett Javelin flat-four engine was tested on the works dynamometer, but was found to deliver less than 50bhp at 3,500rpm, as against the standard 1500 output of 61bhp at 4,000rpm, and 66bhp at 4,500rpm for the fully-prepared racing engine. A Lea-Francis 1½-litre unit was also loaned to the factory.

In reality, despite the facelift, the company had not really resolved its

First appearance in international motor sport after the war. Peter Clark with the Aerodynamic at Chimay for the Grand Prix des Frontieres meeting in May, 1947. The result was third place in the 2-litre sports car class and Clark's comment was 'faster next time' (Klemantaski).

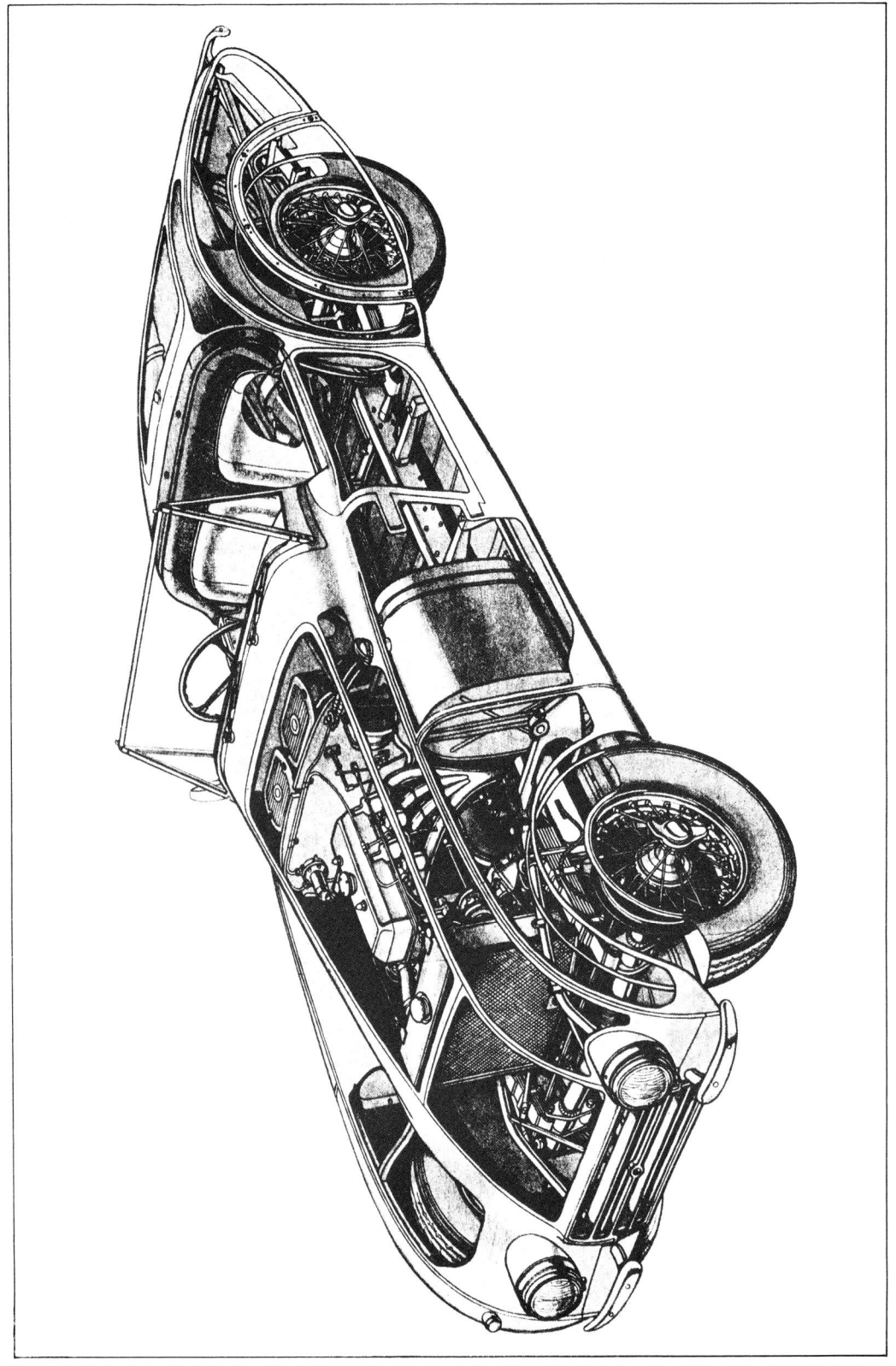

The prototype Aerodynamic in cutaway form. Evident here is the front subframe added to the standard chassis to carry the new body, and the way in which the fuel tank is slung on an outrigger (The Autocar).

basic problems. It was still under-capitalized and the large sales originally envisaged had not come to fruition. In fact, it was general engineering which continued to support the company and the volume of that work increased steadily in the immediate postwar years to 50% of turnover. The Fox & Nicholl business became increasingly unsatisfactory: in 1947 the company came to an agreement with Arthur Fox to terminate the contract, some 31 bodies only having been built, and the Aerodynamic was withdrawn.

An Aerodynamic was taken to Prague for the first postwar motor show in Czechoslovakia, a rather austere affair by the look of it. The car was returned to England after the show. The trophies at the back of the stand were won by Treybal's 1½-litre.

Despite the very difficult conditions experienced in postwar Britain, with petrol in very short supply, motor sport had begun to re-establish itself. The prewar H.R.G. cars had survived and were once again in competition, in the hands of newcomers such as Jack Richmond, A.O. Gosnall and John Newton, who rapidly made his reputation in hill-climbs with the ex-Baillie Hill car, GPB 250, holding the class record at Prescott for several years. Phil Uglow, aided by Ashley Cleave, dominated West Country trials, and their car, now fitted with a 1½-litre Riley engine, also

An export model Aerodynamic as delivered to Switzerland. The driver looks delighted.

79

gave a good account of itself in racing. Ken Delingpole changed from his 1½-litre to a new 1500 and a number of other drivers started cutting their teeth in minor events, including John Gott, Nancy Mitchell and Robin Richards.

Peter Clark had put his name down immediately the Aerodynamic was announced and took delivery of one of the first to be completed. In due course, he disposed of his 1½-litre and joined forces with Jack Scott, also a new Aerodynamic owner, to campaign the cars, which were prepared, as before, by Marcus Chambers. The first international competition appearance of the car was in Clark's hands in the sports-car race of the Grand Prix des Frontieres at Chimay, Belgium, in May 1947. The car went very quickly in the race and might well have won had 'tea leaves' not got into the fuel system, which deprived the engine of 500rpm and dropped it to third place.

As Clark reported: *Otherwise the car ran well and still has the best roadholding, steering and braking of any car on the road. If only we can get that engine to brace its ideas up, we shall have something and I only hope you will not be led astray by the sales department into fitting an inferior IFS.*

Peter had attacked the body rattling problem himself: *It cost over £60 to throw away all the ¼in Whitworth set screws and other coachbuilder's junk with which the car was first assembled and refit with aeronuts as originally specified.*

Other rattles were treated with rubber and Bostik adhesive, but the sounds of the Aerodynamic body had not passed unnoticed in other less competent quarters. *It strikes me*, wrote Clark, *there are too many of them being sold too quickly secondhand.*

In July 1947 Guy Robins took an Aerodynamic on the first postwar Alpine Rally. He retired in the early stages, following a collision with a lorry in Cannes, but the experience gained was to prove valuable the following year.

During the 1946-47 period, a total of 86 cars were produced, including 34 chassis intended for Aerodynamic bodies. But the early demise of what had been intended as the new, big-selling style emphasized the sad fact that the vital question of the design and production of a replacement for the basic two-seater car remained unanswered: the nettle had still not been grasped. As other manufacturers' output increased and new models began to appear, the sales of what was at least a 12-year-old design — some would say considerably older — were bound to diminish.

International success 7
1948

Despite all the problems of manufacturing in postwar Britain, the factory was very busy at the start of 1948, and during the year no less than 44 cars were produced. Both at home and abroad competitions were starting up again on a regular basis and there were a number of international events suitable for the H.R.G. At home, a bout of Crippsian austerity made petrol very hard to come by, but somehow people managed and competed in a wide range of rallies, trials and races.

Peter Clark and Jack Scott had organized a full programme for the two Aerodynamics, to which considerable thought had been given over the winter, developments including the installation of two-way radio. As early as 1939, Clark had proposed radio communication for his 1940 Le Mans entry. The war, while preventing the proposal becoming reality, nonetheless resulted in the production of much improved radio equipment and, for the 1948 season, Clark and Marcus Chambers installed two-way units in both HLO 168 and HXR 530. Pye Telecommunications Ltd were particularly interested in this project, as they were anxious to obtain a supply contract for the Belgian Police Force. When they discovered that the cars were due to run at Spa-Francorchamps, they provided PTC102 sets for Clark's team, similar to those on offer to the Belgians. The set was known to be reliable and was, of its time, light, weighing 37lb.

This substantial four-pack unit had a volume of around a cubic foot and was fitted under the scuttle on the passenger's side in a rubber-mounted cradle. Additional to this was an aerial mounted on the top of the boot, a receive/transmit switch on the dashboard, a headset and a hand-held microphone. The radio operated on fixed frequencies in the 77-83mc/s band. The base set, with a 30ft aerial, had a working range of 5 miles.

The team used the system on three occasions. It was tested at the Manx Cup Race and worked sufficiently well to be used both as a racing aid and a publicity feature at Spa, where Radio Belge broadcast and also recorded the team conversations. For this event, Ray Barrington Brock's car was also equipped with radio and it was justifiably claimed that the radio link played an important part in winning the Coupe du Roi. The system was used again when Clark and Scott took part in the Montlhéry 12 Hours, the recordings in this case being made by the BBC — all very correct, despite the fact that Scott was driving with a major stomach upset necessitating several unscheduled pit stops. The concept of intercom was in front of its time — 30 years or so would pass before its use came to be taken for granted by top sports-car racing teams — and the equipment was sacrificed, during the rebuild of the Clark-Scott team the following winter, in the interests of weight. Undoubtedly there were other potential disadvantages, too, as depicted by Sammy Davis on page 101.

Both Aerodynamics were prepared by May 1948, and were entered at Chimay for the Grand Prix des Frontieres. In the 8-lap, 87km, 2-litre class race, Clark went into the lead pursued by de Sauge's Cisitalia, with Scott in third place. The two H.R.Gs were touching 102mph on the straight, but on the third lap Clark fell back with vapour lock. Despite two pitstops, he finished in fourth place and Scott drove particularly well to finish just 18.7 seconds behind the winning Cisitalia.

In the Isle of Man Manx Cup Race, Clark and Scott, now wired up for

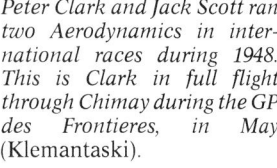

Peter Clark and Jack Scott ran two Aerodynamics in international races during 1948. This is Clark in full flight through Chimay during the GP des Frontieres, in May (Klemantaski).

Clark made two impromptu stops with fuel feed trouble during the Chimay race and is shown here discussing the situation with Marcus Chambers.

radio, were joined by E.W. Holt with his specially-bodied H.R.G. and Folland with Clark's prewar 1½-litre. Holt, with the lightest of the four cars, was 2mph faster than the Aerodynamics, but it was Clark, in sixth place, who set the pace in the race itself. Folland retired early with a broken oil pipe and Scott and Clark had their own private duel until late in the race, when Scott overshot the hairpin. Holt regained some speed and passed both the Aerodynamics, finishing sixth, with Clark seventh and Scott ninth.

It was clear that 'L'Ecurie du Lapin Blanc' needed a third team car for the Spa 24-hour race and this role was filled by an unusual version of the marque.

The factory only ever built one closed H.R.G. — the 1938 coupe — but a

E. W. Holt had a special body constructed to order for his H.R.G. and achieved some success in national competitions.

Ray Barrington Brock with his Aerodynamic-based coupe in the form in which it was originally constructed in 1948 (The Autocar).

second closed car was constructed privately by Ray Barrington Brock in the early months of 1948. Brock had originally ordered an Aerodynamic H.R.G. but, tiring of the delay in delivery, discovered that the chassis could be obtained more or less immediately. He had never built a body before, but decided to have a try and set out his requirements. Firstly, it should be a well-streamlined two-seater which was comfortable to drive. Secondly, it should either be a fixed-head coupe or preferably a coupe de ville. Thirdly, the construction should be as light as possible, with first-class visibility.

The Aerodynamic chassis weighed 1,350lb complete with dashboard and full equipment, including lamps, and Brock was able to acquire many standard Aerodynamic body panels. He also borrowed the factory body jig for a day to set up the front section. The rear section was designed as a separate structure, the front end of which started at the rear door pillar, rising with twin struts connecting the door pillar to the tail in an A-shape, this giving the necessary headroom.

Between the front and rear sections, which each weighed just under 60lb, were the doors, similar in shape to the Aerodynamic's, but very much lighter (9lb each), with Perspex side windows. The doors were fitted with flexibly-mounted locks, which allowed movement between the two structures to take place without the doors flying open. The windscreen and the section over the driver's head proved to be more complicated. The screen was styled similarly to that of the Aerodynamic, but using a lighter framework, and at this stage Brock shelved the idea of a flexible, removable cover as might be used on a coupe de ville, fitting instead a light aluminium roof panel rigidly fixed to the deep section above the screen, but with a

84

The driver's control panel for the radio installation, shown here on the Barrington Brock coupe (The Autocar).

sliding arrangement where it overlapped the rear body section. The rear was located by means of sliding bolts working over an oiled leather strip. An undershield was fitted, this being built of plywood, glued and screwed to a dural frame.

Whilst the construction was in progress, Brock was invited by Peter Clark to join his team for the Spa 24-hour race, for which the car had not necessarily been designed. Air extractors were built into the bonnet panel, which had the effect of reducing the engine temperature by 20°C. Another problem that had to be resolved was that the exhaust pipe, which ran inside the undershield, overheated the cockpit, the undershield having to be redesigned to expose the pipe.

The need to produce really comfortable seats caused some headaches from the point of view of weight, a 2lb frame rising to 20lb by the time it had

Cockpit of an Aerodynamic with the radio intercom installed. Dashboard instrumentation is similar to the standard-bodied 1500 except that no fuel gauge is provided (Pye Telecommunications Ltd).

The three H.R.Gs before the start of the 24-hour race at Spa in 1948 with Clark, Scott and Brock all wearing their earphones.

become a fully-upholstered unit. However, when completed, the coupe weighed 1,687lb as against the conventional Aerodynamic which tipped the scales at 1,710lb.

By now, Clark had become skilled in the complexities of running a racing team, having learnt both by experience and also from the legendary Sammy Davis of Bentley fame. Le Mans was still not on the calendar in 1948, so Clark and Marcus Chambers threw their efforts into the 24-hour race at Spa-Francorchamps, to be run on July 10-11. The arrangements — technical, financial and logistic — were carefully planned and details circulated to the 15-strong party. Marcus Chambers, whose decisions 'must be accepted as law', was team manager in charge of the driver pairings Peter Clark and Pierre Marechal in HLO 168, number 42; Jack Scott and Neville Gee in HXR 530, number 44; and Ray Brock and Dorothy Drydon in the coupe, MPA 792, number 46. Support came from the mechanics Jack Denny, Pat O'Hanlan and Harry Shaw, plus Rosemary Brock, Marie Scott and Brigid Marechal as timekeepers. Ariel Clark was in charge of catering and Ken Custerson was to run the radio communications. Besides the cars, the team's equipment was to be moved in a 3-ton Ford truck and Clark's Bentley Speed Six.

The squad was to set sail the weekend before the race, as there was a busy preparatory programme, including radio tests, an official reception at the Brussels showrooms of H.R.G's Belgian agents — SINCA — not to mention two practice sessions. Everyone was issued with full instructions covering all aspects of the expedition, the first communique ending cryptically: 'On Saturday and Sunday we blow the cars up, on Monday we mend them and on Tuesday night we come home'.

At the end of June, Dorothy Drydon had to withdraw due to illness and her place was taken by Bob Freeman-Wright. Meantime, the team had persuaded the Bank of England to allow a £600 foreign currency allocation for the trip and it was felt that, with a little luck and some prize money, this was sufficient.

Shortly before the team left, a complete schedule was issued covering pit stops, a full procedure having been worked out to cover each car. At a time when pit drill tended to be amateurish at best and frequently plain chaotic, Peter Clark's team set a very high standard. Besides the routine work, the team was driving to a plan, aiming to maintain a predetermined average, in the best long-distance racing tradition, rather than getting drawn into short-term sprint matches with other competitors.

Apart from the fact that Chambers and Marechal were arrested as American army deserters in Brussels — their unlikely alibi of being involved in a motor race finally being verified by a sports-minded policeman — everything, in detail, went well up to arrival at Spa. There, the circuit and its surroundings were almost under water, due to incessant heavy rain, and the paddock was a morass. Practice was duly completed without too many problems, apart from the need to change a head gasket on Scott's car. On Saturday, July 10, the rain fell steadily all morning, but at the start of the race the sky cleared. The respite lasted a very short time and for the remainder of the 24 hours it rained...and rained.

The three H.R.Gs had only one serious opponent in the 1½-litre class, the Scaron/Veyron Simca-Gordini. This car was able to lap nearly 10mph faster than the H.R.Gs and took a 50-mile lead within the first eight hours. A number of cars had retired very early on in the race, including one of the streamlined little 1100S Fiats, which crashed at Eau Rouge, leaving the H.R.Gs well-placed for the team prize. Brock was discussing the situation with Sammy Davis when the latter pointed to HLO 168, which had stopped out on the circuit. Immediate action was taken: the driver Marechal was called up on the radio and he explained that the distributor

Spa 1948: the Scott/Gee car refuelling at dawn. Neville Gee fixes down the tonneau cover while Jack Denny dips the fuel tank (Klemantaski).

Green: Clark-Marechal

On stopping —

(a) Driver opens bonnet catch, switches off ignition and fuel pump.

(b) Driver unplugs headset and gets out of car.

(c) Driver puts helmet on pit counter, takes water funnel and jug.

(d) Driver walks round front of car to N/S and opens bonnet.

(e) Driver tops up with water (if necessary) to within 1in of top (do not overfill).

(f) Driver examines oil flexes for leaks.

(g) Driver checks and oils SU dashpots.

(h) Driver checks security of batteries.

Meanwhile —

(i) Mechanic dips fuel tank, tells pit how many 4-gallon churns required in all, and fills up.

(j) After fuelling, mechanic takes final dip(s), returns· fuel funnel to pit counter and takes up oil bottle.

(k) Mechanic opens oil level tap, checks state of oil flow to valve gear by examination through filler hole, and then puts in normal (practice data) amount.

Meanwhile —

(l) Driver informs him of any repairs needed and then sets off on a tour of inspection of wheels, tyres, shockers and springs.

(m) Mechanic checks pump pulley bracket and belt and shuts bonnet if all okay. Only on completion of all the above will any other work be undertaken.

(n) If no wheel changes are required, driver gets off track and gives new driver any gen.

(o) New driver satisfies himself all properly battened down, gets in car, plugs in headset, switches on the r/t, locks bonnet, switches on ignition and main fuel pump and starts off.

(p) Mechanic advises car's timekeepers of the total fuel on board before and after refuelling.

had come adrift. Fortunately, the earphone lead was long enough for him to lean over the engine and replace and retime the distributor under the instructions of Marcus Chambers. The operation was successful, despite Marechal's knowing very little about the inside of the car, and he was able to drive back to the pits where the job was done properly. Soon after, Chambers was called on to display superhuman powers: Scott's head gasket had blown in practice, now it was Clark's turn. Three times Chambers replaced the head gasket, in 47, 45 and 52 minutes respectively. Each time, as soon as humanly possible, the car was sent out to complete one lap prior to final adjustments, enabling it to qualify by lapping once per hour.

Later on in the race the radio developed a fault with the switches vibrating out of their mountings. There was disintegration on a large scale when the coupe, which had been victim of a stone thrown up by Tommy

Red: Scott-Gee

    Same except —

    (q)   Driver can talk to mechanic whilst latter fills o/s sponson tank first.

    (r)   Mechanic fills second tank while driver inspects tyres, etc.

Yellow: Brock-Wright

    Same except —

    (s)   Driver does water from offside.

    (t)   Mechanic must go round rear of car to get at fuelling hole.

    (u)   Driver checks oil flexes, SU dashpots and battery security after completion of fuelling while mechanic does oil.

Wheel Changes

If wheel changes are required, the routine will carry on from (m) as follows:

    1   Driver knocks cap off and pockets it.

    2   Mechanic lifts car on racing jack.

    3   Driver pulls old wheel off.

    4   Mechanic puts new wheel on.

    5   Driver knocks hub cap on.

Clockwise traffic only round the car throughout, and then resume normal routine.

DO NOT HURRY. Undue haste leads only to mistakes. Do your work smoothly and methodically, and you will get through it much quicker than it would appear. Target time 2 minutes.

Track Discipline

We play this game off against 'bogey' [plan schedule] and pay no regard to other cars unless requested to do so. In order to win, it is necessary to finish. Sixty percent of the starters will not finish. Let them go flashing past, they are welcome.

Wisdom's Healey, lost its windscreen. The glass was carefully knocked out and stowed in the car, to conform to the rules. For a while, the streamlining of the car was highly effective in that a cushion of air was formed in the cockpit so that the driver did not need goggles, despite the rain. However, the buffeting and vibration placed a tremendous stress on the screen pillars and the flexible roof panel, and in the early hours of the morning the top was removed, parcelled up and placed in the car, which now ran in almost coupe de ville trim — with the rear structure acting as an air brake.

Scott's car, which spent only 45 minutes in the pits spread over eight stops during the entire race, was in second place in class, but nearly 200 miles behind the Simca, which was averaging over 71mph. At the 18-hour mark, many of the 'hares' from the earlier part of the race, including the Chiron/Chinetti Ferrari, three 3-litre Delages and the 3.5-litre Delahayes, were out of contention as a result of various mechanical maladies and

Spa 1948: the Barrington Brock car, reduced to coupe de ville form, minus screen and roof, finishes the 24-hour race. Clark and Marechal appear suitably relieved, while the driver takes a well-earned beer (Klemantaski).

accidents in the torrential rain, leaving Scaron in the Simca-Gordini second overall behind the eventual winner, the Aston Martin of St John Horsfall and Leslie Johnson. Later, the French car was delayed in the pits for 20 minutes, but it emerged to run faster than ever. The three H.R.Gs finished without further problems, taking the Coupe du Roi Albert team award from the only other team to finish intact, the 1,100cc Skoda saloons.

Final placings in the 1½-litre class were:

First:	Scaron and Veyron	1,706 miles	71.08mph
Second:	Scott and Gee	1,511 miles	62.96mph
Third:	Brock and Wright	1,425 miles	59.35mph
Fourth:	Clark and Marechal	1,304 miles	54.34mph

Marechal put in the fastest H.R.G. lap at 7 minutes 24 seconds for the 9.01-mile circuit, while the fastest refuelling stop took 2 minutes 57 seconds. The Clark/Marechal car spent just under 4 hours in the pits.

The XI Rallye International Automobiles des Alpes — Criterium de la Montagne, the 1948 Alpine Rally, was a high point in H.R.G's competition career. It was a historic event in its own right, the first of the new style international rallies, rather than a sporting holiday, with British cars out in force. Indeed, this one event sowed the seeds of the great BMC rally team of the 1950s and 1960s, but that is another story. Guy Robins' expedition with the Aerodynamic on the 1947 Alpine convinced him that the event had strong possibilities and accordingly he decided to raise a team. Letters

Belgian H.R.G. agents SINCA made the most of the Spa result and other competition successes, as well as highlighting the pioneering use of radio communication.

were sent to owners known to be interested in competition, suggesting that they might care to combine a continental holiday with some not-too-serious rallying. The seed was sown and fell on fruitful ground. Robins was soon at work on the organization, approaching the Bank of England for special currency allocations, drawing up travel plans and obtaining assistance from the RAC.

As the result of his efforts, no less than eight would-be competitors met at the factory on May 22: John Gott, the Mitchells and A.B. Hunter had Aerodynamics; Jack Richmond his 1500, plus Robin Richards, Rod Ross,

Alpine Rally 1948: Robin Richards removes the rocker box of his 1100 to satisfy the scrutineers at Marseilles (The Motor).

Keith Darby and Peggy Lambert with 1100s. Various knowledgeable people explained the nature — and the difficulties — of the event. While the men were being advised on sundry technical matters, the ladies were also being briefed. Time, it was explained, was of critical importance — so much so that quick-release camiknickers were to be worn to cut down the length of essential stops.

Only Richmond had previously driven in a major rally, only Gott had driven abroad before, but by the end of the day two teams of cars — three 1,500cc cars led by Gott and three 1,100cc cars led by Richards — were organized. Hunter and Miss Lambert elected not to take part. Although the policy of the company was not to field factory teams, the back-up for the Alpine was such that few works teams could have been better supported. The cars and their crews were as follows:

1500 Team

John Gott and Jock Gillespie	JGO 463, number 65
Jack and Mary Richmond	KHN 600, number 66
Doug and Nancy Mitchell	JGJ 76, number 67

1100 Team

Robin Richards and John Beaumont	JGJ 80, number 77
Rod Ross and Ted Farley	JLA 13, number 75
Keith Darby and Guy Ward	HLO 161, number 76

The event was to be run from July 13 to 18, in four stages: Marseilles to Aix-les-Bains, a distance of 285 miles at night; Aix-les-Bains to Lugano, 304 miles; Lugano to Chamonix, 194 miles; and Chamonix to Nice, 388 miles, all in daylight. At Nice, the surviving cars would be checked and would then take part in an acceleration and reversing test. During the stops between stages the cars were to be placed in a parc ferme, where no servicing or maintenance could be carried out.

Preparation for the test at Nice led Robins to arrange a practice session and he made application for a petrol allowance so that the drivers could familiarize themselves with the layout.

He set the ball rolling on April 16 with a letter to the Regional Petroleum Office, but nothing happened until a telegram was sent which produced a reply on May 10. On May 11, Robins managed to get a telephone call through and an 'instant reply' was promised. Again nothing happened, so a week later another telegram was sent and in a day or two this produced telephonic instructions to send a messenger to room number so-and-so at the Regional Office to collect the coupons. Patience rewarded, you imagine? Not a bit of it. The messenger was sent along, waited most of the morning for attention, then was told to return after lunch and, after more waiting, was taken into another room nearby where the occupant was seen to be sitting with his feet on the table reading a newspaper. But there were still no coupons. The gentleman whose labours had been disturbed said it would be quite irregular to give coupons out in that manner and so the messenger came away empty-handed.

Alpine Rally 1948: Robin Richards and John Beaumont check in to a control during their coupe-winning drive (The Motor).

Alpine Rally 1948: Mitchell, Gott and Richmond carrying out routine checks and maintenance (The Motor).

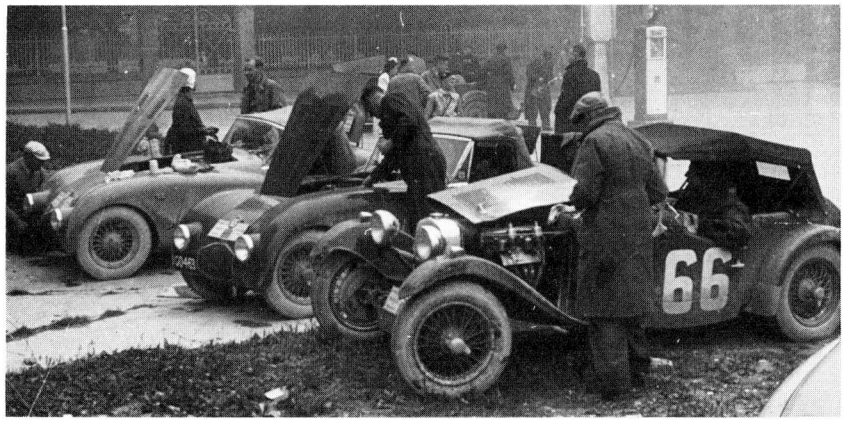

There was a sequel, however, for a day or two later some coupons arrived. They were for about one-sixth of the quantity required; they were also for industrial purposes, such as bench testing. At that point, Robins gave up the struggle, collected the dossier of the case and sent it to the Government Minister concerned personally. The team got their practice in the end!

The cars were prepared at Oakcroft Road and several modifications

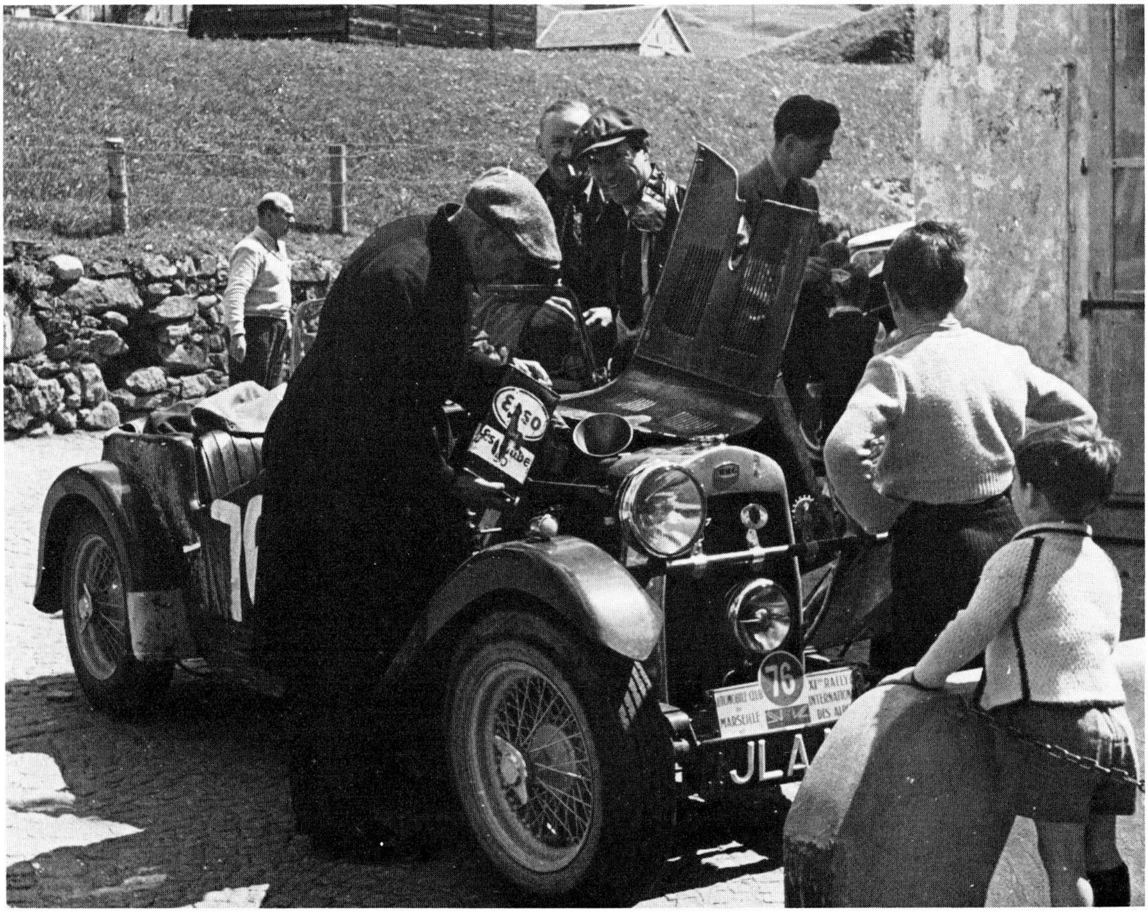

Alpine Rally 1948: Rod Ross tops up his 1100, providing entertainment for various onlooking locals (The Motor).

The Aerodynamic crewed by Doug and Nancy Mitchell high up in typical alpine scenery during the 1948 Alpine Rally (The Motor).

were made. The 1500s were fitted with twin fuel pumps and lines; the 1100s had electric pumps fitted, supplementing the mechanical units. Filters and advance/retard controls were added to cope with the high altitudes and poor-quality French petrol. Louder horns and harder brake linings were used. Darby had his own special modification — his twin spotlamps were set pointing at angles, for going round corners at night. This caused a lot of laughter, but the idea was sound and was found to be highly effective. The decision was taken to carry only running spares, such as hoses, floats, fan belts and the like. The need for more basic items, such as valves, would mean that the car was out of the rally anyway. Every possible detail was meticulously planned and, bearing in mind that most of the drivers and navigators were complete novices, the cars left for Marseilles as well prepared as any and a lot better than some. Not that officialdom was beaten yet: a zealous Customs Officer at Dover insisted that the tape covering the wheel balancing weights was removed. The team might have been smuggling gold.

There were some other subtle moves: Richards drove down through Switzerland inspecting some of the route and, equally important, filling the tank and fuel can with top-quality Swiss petrol. By careful planning and judicious blending with the low-octane French fuel, Richards was able to upgrade his petrol throughout the rally and arrived at Nice with just 2 gallons of pure Swiss petrol, ready for the special test. This was to have its reward.

The cars were scrutineered at Marseilles on July 12 with little difficulty except that the officials of the Automobile Club de Marseilles et Provence were not satisfied that the 1100 water pumps were standard. After some argument, a catalogue was produced and they were satisfied, the key items on the cars being marked to prevent replacement. At this point, Richards' secret weapon was revealed: bicycle inner tubes protruding through the floorboards and extendable up to seat level made it possible for natural bodily functions to be performed without the need to stop.

The rally started at midnight on July 13, the first stage including a timed climb of the 6,000ft Mont Ventoux. This nearly ended in tragedy: Richmond misjudged a particularly difficult left-hander. John Gott was just ahead at the time:

On the lower shoulders of the Ventoux the cars were still in team order, as we could see from our mirror, but after surmounting the 'Wall of Death' all lights vanished and we had a sickening feeling that something had happened. We climbed slowly, not at all reassured by the sight of one of the Simcas which had come to violent grief by the roadside, and it was not until we were about at the summit that we could see '66' and '67' climbing rapidly astern.

At the foot of the mountain we stopped and the others drew up behind.. Jack Richmond announced calmly that he had gone over the top of the 'Wall', but had been pushed back on to the road and continued. Douglas and Nancy Mitchell had arrived at speed in time to see him going over: a

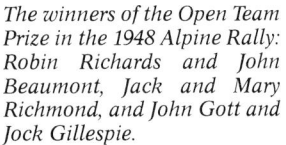

The winners of the Open Team Prize in the 1948 Alpine Rally: Robin Richards and John Beaumont, Jack and Mary Richmond, and John Gott and Jock Gillespie.

At Montlhéry for the Paris 12-hour race in September, 1948. Clark, Scott and Chambers getting into the spirit of the event.

pretty grim sight. I do not think the appearance of the Devil in person would unduly worry Jack, but Mary, who did not know whether the drop was 12 or 1,200 feet, was very shaken, although after some brandy she pluckily agreed to carry on sooner than spoil the team's chances.

(*Motor Sport*, September 1948).

The 1100 team was more fortunate, with Ross taking the cup for the best class performance on the Ventoux, but by the time the cars reached Aix, only Gott and Richards from both the H.R.G. teams were unpenalized. Richmond in particular was having brake difficulties after his excursion.

After resting for a day and night, the cars were off again in pouring rain, the route taking in four major climbs, including the 7,300ft Susten Pass. There was also an unannounced timed climb on the Oberalp, which had to be completed at a given average. The 'secret' climb was chaotic and the test was virtually scrapped, but not before most of the drivers had had phenomenal avoidances and one unfortunate had had his windscreen smashed by an irate cowherd.

At Lugano, the two teams were still intact and there was great amusement when a copy of the *Daily Express*, with a report on the progress of the rally by its correspondent Basil Cardew, appeared on the news-stand. Cardew overdid the purple prose with references to a 'suicide car trial' and a 'night race over the Alps on cart tracks'. 'Cars', he reported, 'were skidding off the road' and had 'torn into trees' or 'just disappeared over the passes'.

From Lugano to Chamonix over the St Gothard and Furka Passes, calamity struck the 1100 team. Darby, who had only dropped 4 points, made a navigational error just after the Furka and, in retracing his steps, lost his road book. Without the vital road book elimination was inevitable and Darby, who had not discovered the loss until later, was disqualified. Meanwhile, Richards' 1100 was suffering from a sheared windscreen wiper drive and shortly afterwards one of the front wing stays fractured. It

Montlhéry 1948: Clark in the Aerodynamic chases the Clapp/ Lilley 1100 (Klemantaski).

was bound up with wire and tyre levers and a friendly garage managed an instant welding operation, but near the Swiss border it snapped again and the wire and tyre levers were replaced. The car was put away in the parc ferme at Chamonix, the proceedings enlivened by the latest *Express* epic, which had the 'suicide squad' driving at 100mph along mountain ledges.

Driving on the last day featured two major climbs, the 9,000ft Col de l'Iseran and the Galibier. Gott, desperately short of petrol and unable to collect more than an absolute minimum, came on an unannounced timed section on the Col d'Izoard and, with his foot hard down, ran out of fuel 20 yards before the finish. The Aerodynamic was pushed over the line, but not before the luckless Gott had accumulated 364 penalty points. He got going

Montlhéry 1948: Thompson, heavily bandaged from the road accident before the race, takes the discretionary line low down on the banking (Klemantaski).

again and the chase to Nice began. Richmond lost more time when the steering column dropped into his lap, the result of a bolt coming loose. Several other drivers crashed. Richards started taking things easy and came within an ace of losing time, but arrived without loss of points to take a Coupe des Alpes. The Mitchells had a seized camshaft and made the final check with a minute to spare.

After resting for a night, the cars were scrutineered on the morning of Sunday, July 18. Richards got away with his wing stay, but had an anxious moment with a sidelamp, which was poorly earthed. Then the cars were put through the special test, accelerating over 333 metres, crossing a line and then reversing to stop astride it. The 1,100cc class, carrying with it the equivalent of a £25 first prize, lay between Richards' H.R.G. and Auriach's

Motor racing began at Goodwood in 1948. Chased by Charles Meisl in his 1500, Gerry Ruddock's Le Mans model H.R.G. finished second in the 1,500cc race at the first meeting, in September.

The 1100 chassis built up by Douglas Hull for Sir Clive Edwards and equipped with a single-seater body and a Lea-Francis engine is seen here at the Brighton Speed Trials, 1948 (National Motor Museum).

Simca, which had also won a Coupe des Alpes, but the H.R.G's fuel and carefully preserved brakes carried the honours.

The five surviving H.R.Gs had thus amassed one Coupe des Alpes, the Coupe de l'Hotel Majestic de Chamonix for the 1,100cc class, as well as two cups won by Richards and Richmond for best class performances in the Nice final tests and Ross' Mont Ventoux cup. Addditionally, the three 1500s had won the foreign make team prize as they were the only three nominated cars to finish. Ross finished fourth in the 1,100cc class and Richmond, Gott and the Mitchells finished third, fourth and fifth in the 1,500cc class.

Just before the prizegiving ceremony, Joe Lowry, covering the rally for *The Motor* was checking the award list when he spotted that the combination of Richards, Richmond and Gott had put up a better performance than the announced winners of the Open Team Award, the Simcas, so the team picked up yet another prize. At the ceremony Mary Richmond collected the Open Team Award, but Nancy Mitchell was forced to call in assistance as the Foreign Team Award was too heavy for her to carry. It was a famous victory, not only for H.R.Gs, but for the British entry, who took four of the eight Coupes des Alpes awarded in 1948.

There was another highly unofficial award, but history is silent as to whether it was actually presented. A suitable bedroom utensil, inscribed in lipstick 'Coupe de Suicide, awarded to Cardew the Cad', was produced — but even then the Press seemed unable to get their act right. Richards, at that time unmarried, was considerably embarrassed by the report that he and 'Mrs Richards' had won a Coupe des Alpes. Such is the price of fame.

The SINCA display at the Brussels Motor Show. SINCA were agents for Singer and Alvis as well as H.R.G. and all three companies' products are on the stand, but it is H.R.G's competition successes that are celebrated on the glass panel.

The Clark-Scott team ended their competition year at the Paris 12-hour race at Montlhéry in September. The event attracted 47 sports car entries, and included in the proceedings was an eight-car-a-side match race between teams entered by the BRDC and their French counterparts the AGACI, the team completing the greatest number of laps in the 12 hours being the winner. Two cars were to be entered in each of four classes and

the BRDC team were represented by the two 1100s of Robin Richards/Eric Thompson and Hugh Clapp/J. Lilley in the 1,100cc class, the two Aerodynamics of Clark/Marechal and Scott/Gee in the 1,500cc class, the Folland/Connell Aston Martin and the Heath/Rolt Alta in the 2,000cc class, and the two Healeys of Johnson/Haines and Wisdom/Black in the 3,000cc class. Against them were ranged two Simca-Gordinis, a Monopole, a Riley, a Meteor, a DB and two Delages. The remainder of the field were mostly French cars and drivers, plus notably the Chinetti/Lord Selsdon Ferrari and the Phillips/Moore MG.

Just before the race, the Richards/Thompson duo were nearly demolished by a drunken French lorry driver who crashed into their non-competing MG but, suitably bandaged up, they were able to start. Both

The rewards. Some of the international trophies won by H.R.G. drivers during 1948, including the cups and other awards from the Alpine Rally, the Coupe du Roi from Spa and the ice bucket from Montlhéry.

Clark and Scott had their radio systems working under the direction of Marcus Chambers and were acting as mobile communications centres for the entire team, after arguing for the best part of two days with the French Postal Authorities to be allowed to use the equipment. All cars were running on the standard French racing fuel, a blend of 60% petrol, 25% ethyl alcohol and 15% benzole, known as Ternaire. The race was to be an all-day event, commencing at 6am on September 12.

The Montlhéry surface was particularly rough and brakes and suspension were in for a hard time. Clark was the first to suffer and after the first hour was virtually brakeless, having shed his normal VG95 linings in favour of some which were found to fade. Scott came in for a replacement gasket and could have done with something similar himself, as he was in acute gastric trouble. The French, meanwhile, had decided to drive the event flat-out and by the 3-hour mark, they had a 12-lap lead. The Alta was the only British car on the leader board.

During the second period, the very fast Veyron/Manzon Simca-Gordini fell out, as did some of the other faster French cars, and the Alta shed a wheel. The British team now took up the running, and at half-distance were 26 laps ahead. The Folland/Connell Aston moved up, albeit 6 laps astern of Chinetti, who was having his own private race, leaving Selsdon to sit out the event in the pits.

The traditionally highly efficient H.R.G. team had an off-day. The timekeepers and signallers were separate from the pits and, despite the radio, communications were less than perfect. Clark in particular suffered as, unaware that he was in a position to challenge for the class leadership, he came in for minor but time-consuming repairs to the rev-counter and dynamo. On the other hand, the Richards/Thompson 1100, assisted in the pits by Doug Orchard, ran like clockwork and was lying ahead of many faster cars.

The French were individually doing very well, but had lost three cars, so that after 9 hours the British lead had increased to 36 laps. The Healeys were suffering badly from a mixture of brake, suspension and transmission troubles and retired, first making sure that the BRDC could not be beaten. The Aston was the first of the match cars home, in third place, behind Chinetti, who won comfortably. Richards and Thompson were 17th, Clark and Marechal 18th, Clapp and Lilley 20th, and Scott and Gee 23rd. The British won the team match by a convincing 69 laps, prompting Clark to note, 'Obviously to get the best out of our drivers we must bash their heads against lorries the day before the race'.

1948 was the year of the international talents, but at home too the cars were notching up an impressive tally of successes in club and national events. John Newton, the Perkins brothers, Holt and Stewart were prominent in hill-climbs; Jack Radbourne, Phil Uglow, Ken Delingpole and Newton were doing equally well in trials, while Phil Scragg, Charles Meisl and Gerry Ruddock were busy in speed events.

The company celebrated in style with a dinner at the end of the season for the international teams. After the meal, each of the drivers was given 10 minutes to pull the legs of all and sundry. By all accounts it was a very good evening — not that some remembered too much afterwards! It was a fitting finale to the year.

Further achievements 8

1949-1950

1949 should have been a bumper year for H.R.G. The marque's competition successes in 1948 were well publicized — the factory even had a basic advertisement into which they inserted the latest victory each month — and at the beginning of the year there was no serious British opposition to match the 1500s. There was not much anywhere else, although Amedee Gordini was known to be at work on a new team of Simca-engined cars. A new model was scheduled from Abingdon, but for 1949 MG relied on their team of TCs.

The production H.R.G. was slightly modified for 1949. The sidescreens were transferred to a flexible pouch mounted vertically behind the fuel tank. There were detail changes to the hood and screens, and further comfort was added by the standard fitting of 'Float on Air' seat cushions. Headlights were also improved by the fitting of double-filament bulbs in place of the previous offside cut-out system. In a period of very limited petrol supply, the angle of fuel economy was stressed in publications, the 1500 being found by *The Motor* to average 49mpg at a constant 30mph.

On the racing side, Clark-Scott Racing Services had a full programme mapped out with a combination of existing and new cars. Over the winter, Marcus Chambers, based at Oakcroft Road, had built up a single-seater H.R.G. chassis for use in the up-and-coming Formula 2 which permitted unsupercharged 2-litre and supercharged 1,100cc engines. The design was virtually standard H.R.G. with a shortened wheelbase (8ft 0½in), into which a four-cylinder Standard Vanguard engine and gearbox was fitted. The engine was linered down to bring it just below 2,000cc and fitted with 8:1 Martlett pistons and twin Solex carburettors. The gearbox, with steering-column change, was three-speed, which effectively meant two-speed during racing. The radiator was set on a frame in front of the front axle. Tyres were 5.00 × 16 front and 5.25 × 18 rear, with a 3.7:1 rear axle.

Peter Clark's Vanguard-powered Formula 2 single-seater H.R.G. in its original form. The quick-release side panel grilles improved engine access. The steering-column gearchange can be seen in the cockpit (Klemantaski).

The single-seater body was built by Cooper at Surbiton, the design featuring the H.R.G. octagon in the radiator grille. It also incorporated extractor louvres which could be unfastened to allow easy access to the engine sides and sparking plugs. Once completed, the car was taken up to Monaco Motors at Watford, where the Clark-Scott team was based for the season.

At the start of the year, Marcus Chambers dropped out of the scene, having taken up a job in East Africa with the ill-fated groundnut project. His place in the team was taken over by John Wyer, a director of Monaco Motors, who was also involved in the other major project — a team of three H.R.Gs to be entered by the 'Ecurie du Lapin Blanc' for Le Mans and other events. Following a very careful study of the AC de l'Ouest regulations, the two veteran Aerodynamics were stripped ready for a complete rebuild. With Le Mans and Spa in mind, a three-car team was essential and so the successful Eric Thompson/Robin Richards pairing was approached. It was decided that Eric should buy a 1500 rolling chassis which had remained unsold at Follett's for a year. An acceptable price was negotiated and the chassis transferred to Watford, where most of the superstructure was removed and returned to the factory for credit.

Peter Clark's car was used as the prototype for the new bodies. By the end of 1948 he had come to the conclusion that the existing Aerodynamic, despite its streamlining, could go no faster. Additionally, the body was heavy and had required quite considerable maintenance. For the new season, he decided to go for ultra-light weight, with fully-exposed wheels, but with a small frontal area. The original idea was to build the body, which was to be cigar-shaped, in the fashion of an elongated Easter egg, so that the top and bottom sections could be detached completely. The only body frame was a rather sketchy bulkhead cage and the panels were hung on to the chassis with Metallastic mountings. The Easter egg concept fell victim to practicality, the 'egg' ending up as a 'galosh'. The aluminium body was in four sections: a nosepiece incorporating the headlamps; an engine and centre section with a bonnet containing a substantial bulge to cover the carburettors; a rear section covering the fuel tank; and a cover surrounding the spare wheel, which lay horizontally on the rear spring bearer tube. Wings were cycle-type, with struts bolted to the chassis, and the obligatory Le Mans 'door' was one and the same as the hinged metal half-tonneau. All the details and particularly the measurements were arranged to conform exactly with the Le Mans rules. The accompanying photographs are largely self-explanatory: the idea was to build a car that would race for 24 hours and hopefully win, and anything not vital to that end was discarded, hence the lack of body frame. The engine had high-compression pistons and head cooling was assisted by fitting sodium-filled valves. A Lucas racing magneto was used. An 18-gallon fuel tank, with twin lines and large racing fillers, fed through twin SU pumps to the carburettors, the driver having a reserve line switch on the cockpit floor.

The three lightweight H.R.Gs at Le Mans for the 1949 race. Left to right, Peter Clark at the wheel of NPB 71 (number 35), Jack Scott in HXR 530 (number 34) and Dick Protheroe in HLO 168 (number 33).

The cars were fitted with large alloy sumps, finned oil filter/coolers and a reserve gallon oil tank which could be switched on from the cockpit to feed the engine. The seats were of wraparound type to give extra support (driving an H.R.G. at racing speeds for 24 hours is hard work for the lower abdomen), and vital tools were carried under the driver's seat. The passenger's seat was strictly ornamental, very little separating the hypothetical passenger's vital organs from the 80amp/hour battery mounted cunningly beneath the leather-covered plywood.

Drawing on Peter's extensive Le Mans experience, everything on the lightweight cars, which scaled 1,365lb (of which the body amounted to just 50lb), was designed with a view to efficiency during the race. All electrical

Peter Clark's car stripped down as the team look for the cracked chassis and anything else that might have fallen off.

circuits were independently controlled, the fuel system was duplicated, every nut and bolt was pinned or self-locking, and every part was adapted for easy access.

HLO 168 was completed in its new form and tested in April. Results would have been even better if Robin Richards had not turned the car over during the trial run, putting himself out of the team with a broken leg and creating considerable extra work for the Monaco mechanics who were paid for their labours on a three-way split between Clark, Scott and Thompson. The place in the team vacated by the damaged Richards was taken by Jack Fairman.

Following the 1948 experiments, radio intercom was again considered, but dropped in favour of weight reduction, besides which Pye had lost enthusiasm for the project. Great attention was given to all aspects of control, support, spares and even sustenance, so when the team was finally installed in the Cafe du Theatre at Le Mans, everything should have been in perfect readiness — which it was not. Practice was notable for all three cars being stripped down and rebuilt. Clark was convinced his chassis had broken en route, while the Thompson car was still being run-in. Pierre Goldschmidt, the Belgian H.R.G. distributor who had taken over many of the preparatory operations, and the head mechanic, Len Haydon, assisted by Dick Protheroe and Jack Denny, contrived to put the cars back together in time for the race. The team pairings were Peter Clark and Mort Morris-Goodall in HLO 168, number 33; Jack Scott and Neville Gee in HXR 530, number 34; and Eric Thompson and Jack Fairman in NPB 71, number 35.

The most important opposition did not materialize. Gordini was not

Le Mans 1949: the Thompson/ Fairman car during a routine pit stop. One plombeur is sealing the radiator cap, while the second waits for the refuelling to be completed.

ready yet, so the challenge came from the two DBs driven by Lachaize, Debille and the builders of the cars, Deutsch and Bonnet, plus the special MG TC driven by George Phillips and 'Curly' Dryden. In the larger classes the major contenders were the Talbots, Delages and Delahayes, the Chinetti/Lord Selsdon Ferrari and the team of new Aston Martin DB2s. In all, there were 51 starters.

The traditional start at 4pm left Thompson on the line with a flooded engine, but he recovered in fine style. Within the first hour, Clark came in with a defective top water hose and he was left with very little coolant with which to complete a further 7 laps before the seals could be broken and repairs effected. He drove on until the engine seized at Mulsanne and then made his way on foot back to the pits. Morris-Goodall, a water bottle stuffed in his overalls, returned to the car and actually succeeded in getting it moving again, but not for long enough. The car was finally abandoned at 5.30pm.

Thompson handed his car over to Fairman, who was fortunate to find that he had a more flexible spare water hose in his trousers and, shortly after, both surviving cars were fitted with these replacements.After 4 hours, '35' was in 24th position and '34' in 25th, trailing the two DBs, which were running in 13th and 21st positions, the leader being 4 laps up already. The MG was a few seconds in front of the H.R.Gs, but later in the evening Thompson got ahead. Later still the MG was eliminated for having contravened a technical regulation and by midnight '35' had moved ahead of the second DB.

Between 2 and 3am the Scott/Gee car was in the pits having a head gasket changed, but the problem was more basic and after a few more laps '34' was retired with a cracked block. At 4am Fairman handed over to Thompson with the remaining car up into 14th place, 6 laps astern of the Deutsch/Bonnet DB. By 10am it was 13th. Sadly, three hours later, a former member of the H.R.G. team, Pierre Marechal, crashed his Aston Martin and received fatal injuries.

When Fairman took over for his next stint, he recalled later: *Eric warned*

Le Mans 1949: Thompson on his way to the class win. The 18in wheels and high axle ratio gave a maximum speed of about 106mph (Klemantaski).

me there was precious little brake left. He had not exaggerated and going down the straight after a couple of laps I fiddled with the manual adjuster that sticks through the floor to see if there was any more there, but there was not. I remember my sleeve catching in the handle as I straightened up from the operation and the thing must have spun back a couple of turns without my realizing it, for when I arrived at Mulsanne at full chat there was no brake at all worth mentioning. This is a corner that must be respected, so I simply went on down the escape road where I stopped and sorted out the adjuster. This only took about 2 minutes, but it was enough to cause some heart attacks in the pits when the precious remaining car failed to appear on time.

In the closing stages of the race there was considerable excitement in the H.R.G. pit as it became apparent that the leading DB had begun to tire and had spent some time in the pits. Eventually it came to a halt at the start of the Mulsanne Straight. A lap later it had got going again, but only as far as the end of the straight. By the end of the lap, its lead of 10 laps had been whittled away and Fairman had now only to finish to take the class. Fortunately, all went well for the H.R.G, whereas many cars retired during the last few hours in the blistering summer heat. With 10 minutes to go, the pit hung out a 'slow down' sign, which, after nearly 24 hours, Fairman misread as a 'speed up' instruction, taking off as fast as possible and only realizing his mistake half a lap later. The H.R.G. came home at an average speed of 70.84mph, having covered a fraction over 1,700 miles to finish in 8th place overall.

Le Mans 1949: Eric Thompson and Jack Fairman, seen here with two very happy plombeurs, finished 8th overall and first in the 1,500cc class.

The team for the 1949 Spa 24-hour race — the three light-weights of Clark, Scott and Thompson, and the Aerodynamic coupe (Autosport).

Following the Le Mans race, the cars were taken to Brussels, where they were rebuilt at Andre Pilette's garage, Pilette taking over Gee's role as second driver to Scott for the 24-hour race at Spa-Francorchamps. For Spa, the team was joined by Ray Brock and Bob Wright with the Aerodynamic coupe which had been rebuilt and improved since the previous year. The conventional rear suspension had been taken off and the springs replaced by trailing arms and a Watt linkage, with special oil-filled shock absorber struts, pressurized by carbon dioxide, which could be adjusted. The system had been in use on the car for some months and appeared to very suitable for the rough surface at Spa, but it had not been tested under racing conditions. The car was also fitted with Firestone tyres, unlike the rest of the H.R.Gs, which were shod with Dunlops. Brock persuaded Firestone to produce some special tyres suitable for long-distance racing and this they did on a strictly experimental and unofficial basis. This time the opposition was out in force, headed by three Simca-Gordinis and three Fiat saloons, with the Wisdom/Hume Jowett Javelin running as a 1½-litre touring car. Chinetti, with the 2-litre Ferrari, was favourite to 'win' the race, although the event was run in classes only, with no award for best overall performance. However, the two Gordinis took the lead and stayed there, while the H.R.Gs were busy scrapping amongst themselves to the point where Pierre Goldschmidt had to bring Thompson and Pilette to order.

After racing for just over an hour — this year the weather was considerably kinder — Brock came in with rear suspension problems. Under racing speeds on the rough surface, the oil in the new struts was frothing and ineffective so it had to be replaced. Brock was forced to repeat the draining and refilling operation eight times during the race, though fortunately the task could be carried out quite quickly.

By dawn the following day the race and particularly the uneven road began to exact its toll. The bodywork on the cars of both Thompson and

110

Scott started to break up. The Gordinis slowed and finally retired and the Fiats were also in trouble, leaving the battered H.R.Gs in a good position to win the principal award — the Coupe du Roi Albert for the best team performance — for the second successive year. All seemed well, with the Thompson/Fairman car leading the class, when Morris-Goodall came in with piston trouble. After a lengthy pit stop the car staggered away on three cylinders. Shortly afterwards the radiator mountings on Scott's car broke away and the fuel tank on Thompson's car dropped on to the back axle. The Scott car was jury-rigged and after half an hour of hard work with rope and a broomstick, Thompson was away again, still in the class lead, but having lost ground to Brock, who as an independent was not under team orders and might be tempted to 'have a go'. Brock in the meantime was lapping regularly on the road, but was being held back by the need to stop frequently and replace the shock absorber oil. Clark and Brock

Spa 1949: Eric Thompson (number 44) and Andre Pilette (number 46) enjoying their own private race, with the Brock coupe in close attendance (Klemantaski).

Spa 1949: Thompson, during the later stages of the race, with the fuel tank and rear body section firmly lashed together.

Spa 1949: Morris-Goodall waits to start his hourly lap to qualify as a finisher. The broken front wing mounting lashed up with rope was the least of the car's problems (Klemantaski).

discussed the matter and agreed that it was best not to stage a contest at this stage when so much was at stake and all four cars were in various degrees of difficulty.

Towards the end, Clark circulated once an hour to conform to the rules. Meantime, the Brock/Wright coupe had moved into second place, with Scott third.Up ahead, Chinetti was leading the St John Horsfall Aston Martin. With the end in sight, Chinetti rolled the Ferrari but, with considerable outside assistance, the car was got back on to its wheels and he held on to win from Horsfall, who had driven the 24 hours single-handed.

At Spa, the regulations were much more relaxed than at Le Mans. Eric Thompson's last spell at the wheel was typical of the relaxed atmosphere prevailing: *I discarded my goggles and helmet and put on a peaked cap but,*

Spa 1949: the team pose with the spoils of victory, having won the Richard Seaman, Winston Churchill and King Albert trophies. Left to right, Eric Thompson, Jack Fairman, Mort Morris-Goodall, Pierre Goldschmidt, Peter Clark, Andre Pilette and Jack Scott.

unfortunately, on the straight the wind whistled it off my head. To my amazement on the next lap round a gendarme was holding out a long fishing rod over the road and dangling on the end was my cap. I collected it at speed and thereafter we saluted each other every time the car came round.

The H.R.G. team duly finished in one piece — just — finishing 1-2-3-4 in the class and taking the team prize as well as the Coupe de la Victoire for the best-placed British car and driver, and the Richard Seaman Cup for the best-placed British driver. Richly deserved as these trophies were, it was a little hard on Wisdom and Hume, who had driven an uneventful race — though Hume broke a finger in the glove box of the Javelin — to finish in

front of the H.R.Gs on the road, only to have the organizers decide that the Javelin, as a touring car, did not really count. Brock's faith in his Firestone tyres was fully repaid, the car running for the 24 hours on the single set.

The class results were:

First:	Thompson and Fairman	1,564 miles	64.39mph
Second:	Brock and Wright	1,329 miles	55.39mph
Third:	Scott and Pilette	1,177 miles	48.99mph
Fourth:	Clark and Morris-Goodall	1,051 miles	47.92mph

On the home front, the road cars were successful in all forms of competition. There were eight premier award performances by H.R.Gs on the Land's End alone. Gerry Ruddock was particularly successful in club events with the old Le Mans model H.R.G, but the Clark single-seater was

The Brock Aerodynamic coupe after the 1949 Spa race, showing the set of Firestone tyres which lasted the whole event, and also the sliding joint in the top panel, rebuilt after the 1948 outing (G. A. Herbert).

Alpine Rally 1949: Jack
Richmond, 1500, finds time for
a chat with the driver of a
Jowett Javelin (The Motor).

disappointing. It ran at the Easter Goodwood meeting, finishing well down the field. In May, the car was entered for the Manx Cup which, if nothing else, was an opportunity for Clark to display his resourcefulness: *In practice I bounced so much on the back leg that I finally and utterly demolished the seat which had to be reinforced for the race with a lump of galvanized iron which we had to purloin with tin snips by dead of night from the outdoor '...house' of the pub.*

Despite these measures, Clark had trouble with the throttle pedal and, towards the end of the race, the transmission failed. At the Blandford meeting in August, the engine overheated. Certainly, the car, which notionally developed 76bhp at 5,100rpm, was no match for the other early Formula 2 contenders, such as the agile 1,100cc Coopers or even the elderly Rileys. In fact, Hugh Clapp's H.R.G. 1100, fitted with a supercharger, was no less competitive. Surprisingly, the Standard-Triumph organization took an interest in the car and supplied a number of

Alpine Rally 1949: Robins and Brookes take advantage of an enforced stop at a level crossing near Turin to check the 1500. Shortly afterwards, the head gasket failed (The Motor).

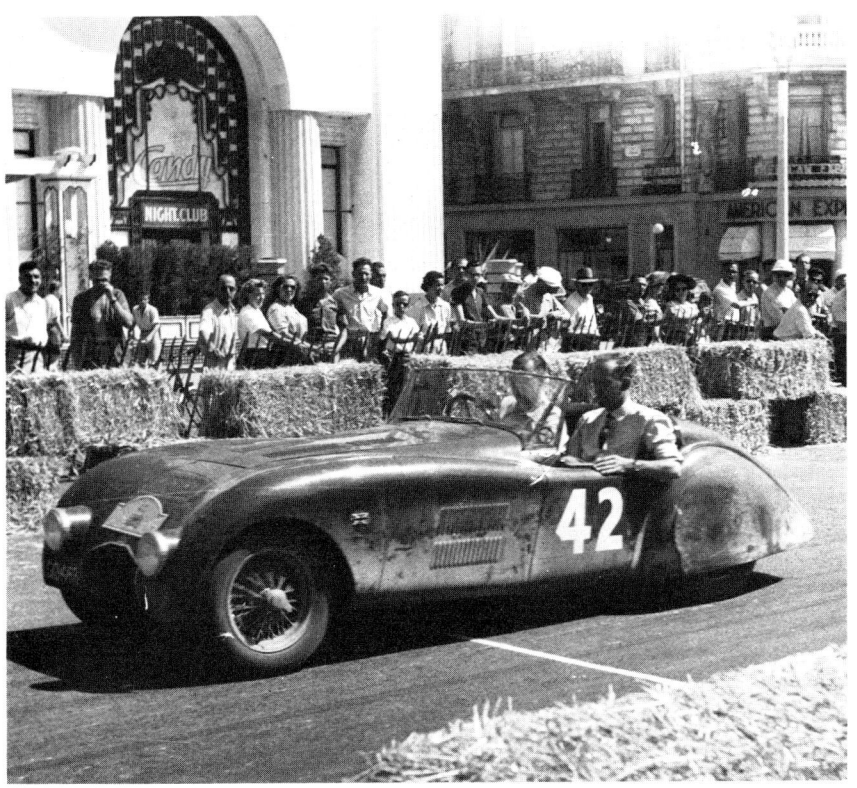

Alpine Rally 1949: Gillespie, Nancy Mitchell and Gott servicing JGO 463, Gott's car, on its second Alpine foray (The Motor).

Alpine Rally 1949: the Gott/Gillespie Aerodynamic reverses astride the finishing line in the special test at Nice (The Motor).

Variation on a theme. The 1500 built for Betty Haig had a subtly modified body constructed by Automarine. The windscreen is raked much further back than normal.

items for it. They were particularly pleased that, whereas they were being pressured to provide large funds for the BRM project which had still not appeared, Clark had used their own components with no funding whatsoever.

Following the successes of the previous year, an even larger squad was assembled for the 1949 Alpine Rally. This time there were two 1500 teams, plus three independents.

Number 1 team

John Gott and Jock Gillespie	JGO 463, number 42
Doug and Nancy Mitchell	NPC 532, number 40
Jack Richmond and Geoff Aspell	KHN 600, number 41

Number 2 team

Guy Robins and Ray Brookes	MPG 177, number 43
Bill Shepherd and John Williamson	GFG 692, number 48
S. Hansen	EH-13-76

Independents

John Roberts	KLD 447, number 49
Rod Ross	JLA 13, number 10
Fred Latimer-Jones and Douglas Leese	JYK 141, number 11

With the exception of Hansen, who lived in Portugal, the drivers had their cars prepared at the factory. In addition to the modifications of the previous year, some new special fittings were organized — improved filters, crossbars to enable the radiator caps to be opened quickly and holes in the bonnet side panels to aid cool-air breathing to the carburettors.

The wings on Betty Haig's 1500 were to her own specification and helped to give the car its own distinctive appearance.

Gott, having found that the Aerodynamic boiled on the long climbs, removed the undershield and took the slats off the radiator grille, replacing them with wire mesh. The Mitchells solved the problem more effectively by buying an open two-seater. The cars really were works-supported on this occasion, with Doug Orchard at the wheel of the company Ford van laden with spares.

The event had attracted a total of 90 entries, no less than 27 of them in the 1½-litre class, with formidable opposition from the MG TCs. The route, which in 1948 had only been through the French and Swiss Alps, had been lengthened to take in the Dolomites, including an 80-mile run on the Autostrada. There were to be timed tests on the Autostrada, the Stelvio and the Vars.

The rally was run in five stages. The first, from Marseilles to Monte Carlo, a distance of 378 miles, was again run at night, including the Ventoux climb. The Number 1 team and Robins went through clean, but Hansen was out with overheating problems on his Aerodynamic, Roberts got lost and ran out of time, the Shepherd/Williamson car was involved in an accident with a taxi which was taking a mountain corner on the wrong side of the road, and Latimer-Jones was afflicted with enteritis and could not continue.

The second stage, 446 miles from Monte Carlo to Cortina, virtually wiped out everyone's clean sheets. Gott, 6 minutes down, was in the class lead. On the Autostrada test he was second fastest in class at 77.8mph, with Ross in the 1100 at 59.7mph. One of the horns on Jack Richmond's car fell off, damaging the radiator, while Guy Robins retired with a blown head gasket. Finally, Ross lost his way and ran out of time.

The H.R.G. team at Silverstone, August 1949. Left to right, Peter Clark, Eric Thompson and John Buncombe. The factory Ford van, support vehicle from the Alpine, is in attendance.

The third stage, 188 miles around Cortina, saw the demise of another H.R.G.— the Mitchells also had head gasket trouble. On the Stelvio test, Richmond put up best performance in class, followed by Gott, but the H.R.Gs were now being harried by the TCs of Betty Haig and Edney, whose better braking compensated for their inferior roadholding. When Gott's petrol tank split, reducing its capacity to around 4 gallons, Miss Haig took over the class lead.

By the time the drivers reached Chamonix, after 402 miles on the 4th stage, there were only 36 survivors of which two — Gott and Richmond — were in H.R.Gs. Edney was pressuring Gott for class 2nd place and took it over when, at the top of the 6,000ft Col de Groux de Fer, the H.R.G's engine cut out with vapour lock, the petrol literally boiling in the lines.Using a snow poultice, Gott cooled the fuel and the car redeemed itself to take best

Silverstone 1949: John Buncombe flat out in the production-car race (Klemantaski).

performance on the Vars climb with Richmond in 4th position.

In the end there were just 31 finishers at Nice. Gott (310 points lost) and Richmond (360) were 3rd and 4th in the class behind the MGs of Miss Haig and Edney, and only one driver — Gautruche, with a Citroen — claimed a Coupe des Alpes in what was truly a test to destruction. Richmond just made it: Aspell had to push the car backwards astride the line on the final special test, the reverse gear having collapsed. The historian, looking back at the event, might be tempted to see the 1949 Alpine as clear evidence of MG superiority — were it not for the fact that Betty Haig promptly ordered a 1500 for herself.

The event also provided an example of H.R.G. service at its most inspired. Miss Lambert was driving her 1100 on holiday in Switzerland at the time. She damaged the front axle in an accident, telegraphed the factory to send a replacement as quickly as possible and left the car parked in a village square. Later in the day she returned — to find it completely

rebuilt! Only afterwards did she discover that Doug Orchard, following the rally in the works van, had contacted the factory and heard of her trouble. He made a detour, replaced the axle using rally spares and went on his way.

The *Daily Express* Trophy Meeting at Silverstone on August 20 featured a production-car race to run for one hour. The event attracted teams from Frazer-Nash, Allard and others, including three new Jaguar XK 120s and three new sports Healeys. The 1½-litre class featured three works TC MGs, two Jowett Javelins, an 1,100cc Morgan, plus three H.R.G. 1500s driven by Peter Clark, Eric Thompson and John Buncombe and an 1100 driven by Hugh Clapp.

On first practice the three H.R.Gs, led by Thompson in his new 1500, dominated the class with an average speed of over 79mph. By second practice on the Friday the suspension and roadholding of the TCs were much improved by the use of vast quantities of heavy tape on the springs, and it was clear there would be a good race. In the best scrutineering traditions, the definition of 'production' was in doubt and an objection was

Silverstone 1949: Eric Thompson passes the TC of George Phillips, the H.R.G. looking much more stable than the MG. Hurg owners were quick to point out the difference.

H.R.Gs featured strongly in Australian motor sport during the late 1940s. Car number 24 in this bunch is one of the Bathurst single-seaters built up from the batch of chassis sold through Brown & Dureau.

The experimental Bristol-engined chassis. Clearly evident is the unusual rear suspension layout, with the standard semi-elliptic H.R.G. spring converted to a cantilever arrangement rather reminiscent of an early Lanchester or even a Silver Ghost!

lodged by Morgan that the H.R.Gs had not been carrying their full road equipment. The scrutineer gave the H.R.G. team until 8am the following morning to rectify the matter and replace the windscreens and sidescreens, which had been removed. Late on Friday, a telephone call was made to Grace Leather asking her to get the missing sidescreens to Silverstone. With the mechanics and others with cars already at the track the only solution was to enlist the assistance of a friend and, leaving at 4am, they just had time to talk themselves into the paddock with the vital screens. In the end a typically British compromise was reached: the cars raced without their windscreens, but carried their sidescreens.

The race started in the Le Mans style and the three XKs soon left the field far behind. Thompson led the class first time round, followed by Buncombe, two TCs and Clark. By half-time, Jacobs' TC got past Buncombe and was closing slightly on Thompson when the MG's throttle pedal stuck down at Becketts, dropping him back following a contretemps with the straw bales. Peter Morgan's Morgan moved up and in the end the order was Thompson, Clark, Morgan and Buncombe, an excellent result

120

for the team. The Healeys took the team prize, in honour of which the model became known as the Silverstone.

Total H.R.G. production in 1949 was 25 cars, compared with 44 the previous year. Even this hides the fact that the sales were considerably enhanced by shipment of 10 rolling chassis, notionally Aerodynamic, to Australia. The company had made a few sales there previously, including two 1100s, and the racing driver Tony Gaze had taken out an Aerodynamic in 1947. After using it in competition, Gaze stripped the body in 1948 and installed a lightweight two-seater, using 18swg aluminium over $\frac{1}{2}$in square steel tubes. This was christened the Woodside and was built by Head Bros of Murrumbeena, in Victoria. Despite the unsuitability of the suspension for other than Australian city roads, the design attracted buyers and Brown & Dureau Ltd, of Melbourne, arranged to import two batches of five chassis. Pistons giving various compression ratios were fitted by the factory, including 7:1, 8.9:1 and 9.25:1. Possibly two Woodside-bodied cars were produced, plus another two single-seater Bathurst models, which were campaigned very successfully by Stan Jones and Lou Molina. The single-seaters, whose compression was raised even further (one appears to have been supercharged), were capable of well in excess of 100mph, but their reliability suffered with dire results, so that replacement engines — Holden and other makes — were installed, and there were a number of dramatic accidents. The remaining chassis were bodied in various ways: the original Aero body off Gaze's car was fitted to one, and

Front end of the Bristol-engined chassis. Similar transverse leaf spring IFS was later used on the twin-cams. The main chassis members are boxed, not channel section.

Blandford 1950: Dick Jacobs clips the grass with the quasi-works MG TD in pursuit of Thompson's 1500. Behind, Buncombe harries Sparrow's Morgan, closely followed by two TCs (Klemantaski).

later another was bodied as a replica two-seater. One chassis was never used at all, but recent research indicates that, from a total of 13 cars and chassis shipped to Australia in the period 1947-52, nine survive in part or in whole.

One further chassis eventually found its way to Sydney, where it also remained unused for many years. This was the experimental design which the company produced to accommodate the Bristol 2-litre engine, using largely standard H.R.G. parts. The chassis was of normal section, but boxed, with the sidemembers at the rear taken up over the rear axle. The front suspension was independent and the brakes were hydraulically-

operated Alfins. Several companies, notably AFN and Cooper, were working on similar projects and the development got no further. The engine, which was on loan from Bristol, was returned, this being the nearest the company ever got to the proposal to include a 2-litre in the range.

Throughout the 1949-51 period, an extraordinary correspondence broke out in the motor sporting press on the relative merits of H.R.Gs and MGs. It all started when a Mr Butts wrote a letter to *Motor Sport* (June 1949) to state that he thought the H.R.G. was an overrated car. Mr Butts quite clearly knew very little about H.R.Gs, or he may have had his tongue in his cheek; anyway, the correspondence columns exploded. Everybody who was anybody — Gott, Clapp, Betty Haig, to name a few — waded in, until *Motor Sport* finally closed the correspondence nine months later. Shortly afterwards, it flared up again in *Autosport*, but in this case it also compared the TC and TD models, with a spot of Jowett Jupiter thrown in for good luck. What it proved was that the H.R.G. and the MG, in their different ways, were both very good, but it did serve to polarize interest in the competitive performances of the two marques, giving the 1950 competition season, in particular, a special extra edge.

The new TD MG was now ready to challenge the 1500s and the two met for the first time at the Blandford Whit-Monday race meeting. Thompson and Buncombe had their 1500s as raced in the 1949 Silverstone race, and Jacobs had what was, unofficially, a works MG entry. Thompson and Jacobs fought it out wheel-to-wheel in the opening laps of the production-car race, but Jacobs took a clear lead on the 10th lap after Thompson had survived an excursion into the bushes. The TD came home first, but the race was awarded to Thompson on a technicality: the TD had a non-production sports coil fitted and this was protested by another MG driver.

The next meeting between the marques was on the 1950 Alpine Rally. There were 27 entries in the 1½-litre class, including many MGs, although none of them works-entered. This year, H.R.G. were represented by four 1500s and three 1100s:

Bill Shepherd and John Williamson	GFG 692, number 50
John Gott and Jock Gillespie	JGO 463, number 51
Jack Richmond and Jim Blumer	KHN 600, number 67
Doug and Nancy Mitchell	NPC 532
Dave Price and Wood	OPE 30, number 32
Rod Ross and Everest	JLA 13, number 28
Epps and Epps	JCD 853, number 29

After the 1949 event Gott had taken his car to the factory to have the Aerodynamic shell removed and replaced by a sports two-seater body. Problems set in from the very start of the expedition. By the time the cars had reached Folkestone, several were in trouble with low oil pressure and urgent repairs were needed. It was Saturday night and there was nobody to answer the frantic telephone call to the factory. Gott, however, managed to contact Grace Leather's brother who, in turn, found Grace. They then set out to find Doug Orchard, who was out at the cinema. The cinema manager flashed up a message on the screen and an apprehensive Orchard came to the foyer. After collecting the necessary spares, the Leathers, Harry Chapman and Doug Orchard left for Folkestone to find the competitors at dinner having great faith in someone's ability to rectify the trouble. Orchard and his amateur mechanics worked through the night tracing the failure to some new oil pipe which, although flexible, was not air-tight. The

Peter Clark with MPG 177 in the Production Car Race, Silverstone 1950. The apparently split tonneau, above the door, allowed the hood to be raised without the necessity of removing the cover.

Dundrod TT 1950. A youthful Stirling Moss, on his way to victory in the Jaguar XK 120, overhauls John Buncombe's 1500 which finished 4th in the 1,500cc class.

competitors left the following morning with oil pressure restored, while four weary persons made their way back to Tolworth — only two of them even being officially involved with the company! The remainder of the journey was rather less traumatic, but just before the start the Mitchells were called home owing to a family illness, leaving the two teams of three.

The rally had been extended to six stages for 1950. The first stage went well and Richmond took the class award for the best performance on the Autostrada at 79.5mph. Before long Gott was revisited by his Alpine bogey, fuel trouble: once again the fuel tank had split. For the next 1,200 miles Gillespie navigated with a pair of 2-gallon petrol cans between his knees, changing them for full spares on the roll. Despite this the car made fastest class time on the Stelvio, backing up Bill Shepherd, who was really making the running, holding joint 1st place in class with a clean sheet.

This year the timed climbs had a special significance in that any car achieving a time more than 5% slower than the fastest in class was penalized. Gott's performance on the Stelvio had caught several MGs, so the two planned a grand-slam finish on the Vars, the aim being to penalize the entire class, giving Shepherd a clear lead. Sadly, the plan backfired: Gott's time was over 5% quicker than every car in the class bar one, but that one was not Shepherd. Halfway up a coil lead vibrated off his car and that was the end of the clean sheet, dropping him to 5th place. Gott eventually finished 8th. Of the 27 starters, only 13 finished. Epps' gearbox failed on the 3rd stage, as did Richmond's. Ross' shock absorbers broke up on the final stage, but Dave Price overcame steering problems to finish 4th in the 1,100cc class, with best performance in class on the Stelvio and the Vars. The MG TDs of Kenk and Keller took 1st and 2nd places in the class, both well-penalized: from now on, winning a Coupe des Alpes with a 1½-litre car was going to be quite a task.

The next encounter between the H.R.Gs and the MGs was at Silverstone, with the three works TDs of Dick Jacobs, George Phillips and Ted Lund, plus Lester's TC, ranged against no less than six 1500s and an 1100. The 1500s were in two groups: the 'racers' comprising Peter Clark, Nancy Mitchell and Tom Christie; and the 'Alpiners' John Gott, Bill Shepherd and Jack Richmond, together with Dave Price's Alpine 1100. This arrangement had to be adjusted when it was made known that the sponsors were not overkeen on the possibility of a lady being involved in an accident, which would be very bad publicity. The net result was that Gerry Ruddock took over Nancy's car.

For 1950 the hour-long production-car race was split into two separate events, for cars under and over 2 litres, but any reduction in the speed differential was minimal as the field included two 2-litre Ferraris driven by Ascari and Serafini. In the melee of the Le Mans start, Gott tried to climb into Richmond's similar green 1500. Ruddock put his nose in front, followed by Christie, but soon Jacobs was challenging for the 2nd place. Clark, with MPG 177, and Grimley, on the Jowett Jupiter, were contesting 6th spot. Christie and Jacobs proceeded to pass and repass for most of the hour, Ruddock holding his lead to win the class at 71.78mph. Just before the finish, Christie's engine expired at Club Corner, letting through Lund and Phillips, followed by the Jupiter and Peter Clark, who shed his spare wheel. Gott was first of the rallyists, in 7th place.

Although there were still several major successes to come, the 1950 TT at Dundrod effectively marked the end of the 1500 as a force in international sports-car racing. Three 1500s, driven by Peter Clark, John Buncombe and A.P. Hitchings, were matched against the works MG TDs, backed up by a bevy of privately-entered TDs and TCs. In practice, the 1500s were running well and Clark was timed, hood erected, at just on 100mph on the Deer's Leap section. As Peter later recalled, it felt like a vertical dive off Beachy Head! The class had a very tough handicap, being set to lap at 74mph and giving away 1.7mph to the 1,250cc MGs, which were in the hands of Jacobs, Lund and Phillips once again.

As the race started, the heavens opened and Clark, who as usual had made a very thorough study of the regulations, realized that this could be helpful to the H.R.Gs. However, since he had last driven the works demonstrator, MPG 177, at Silverstone, the car had been sold and had to be borrowed back for the race. *As it was not my car,* he explained, *I had not thought it appropriate to request one of my special tuning mods, namely, the bodily removal of the handbrake ratchet. Needless to say, in due course, when we were lapping even better than planned, the ratchet engaged itself as we approached the hairpin turn after Wheeler's Corner and nothing on earth — short of dismantlement for which I had no tools — could persuade it to come free.*

It was an inglorious conclusion to Peter Clark's last race in an H.R.G. John Buncombe paddled home 4th in class after the three works TDs, at a little over 60mph, with Hitchings just behind him. The outright winner was a young man — not quite 21 — called Stirling Moss, in a Jaguar XK 120.

The Jaguar's success signalled very clearly the accelerating development of the sports car — not just of one-off competition machines or limited-production exotics, but of cars intended to be widely available. The TD looked very like the TC at a glance, but under the skin a stiffer chassis, independent front suspension and rack-and-pinion steering marked MG's move into the new era. It could only be increasingly difficult for a basically prewar design to compete, on the track or in the market place. Just 13 new cars left the H.R.G. factory in 1950. In every sense it was time for a change.

Changing times

1950-1954

9

For some time, the successes on the circuits and rally routes of what was an elderly design had been masking a growing crisis of identity at Oakcroft Road. The scheme agreed by the directors had been to revitalize the 1940 plans: specifically, Godfrey would go ahead with the design of a new model whilst Robins would continue with the existing production until the new car was ready. As time progressed, however, it became increasingly clear that the new model was not forthcoming and Robins was finding that the production of the basically prewar cars was becoming increasingly difficult. In any case, the market for the 1100s and 1500s was dropping off, but the decreasing sales were being offset by an increase in general engineering work, notably in the field of mechanical handling. Although the industry was still in its infancy, Robins was convinced that there was a large potential market for this equipment and the company worked closely with Smith's Jacking Systems and Lansing Bagnall.

Robins' ideas were not altogether shared by other board members. Selsdon and Mathieson were anxious for car production to remain of primary importance and the conflict of interests was heightened by Robins' view that Godfrey's design work should be carried out separately from the manufacturing side and be handled in the same way as an engineering contract — when the development was completed (and only then) it could be handed over, complete with relevant information and drawings, to the factory for production. This was not Godfrey's way of working, and Robins, after much discussion, resigned early in 1950 to develop his interests in the mechanical handling market, first as a consultant and then as part of Mechanical Handling Ltd.

The departure of Robins had very little immediate effect and Eadington proved well capable of managing the production side. General engineering contracts were maintained and continued to provide nearly half the sales of the company. However, whilst the day-to-day business was covered by Godfrey and Grace Leather, it was clear that the firm's car-making role was slipping away, with no new design anywhere near readiness.

The board decided therefore to find a person to work with Godfrey on the design of a new model, someone who would also be able to take over

Stuart Proctor, Ron Godfrey and Grace Leather, photographed outside the office at Oakcroft Road. Proctor was an old associate of Godfrey's but a new recruit to H.R.G.

development if and when Godfrey retired. The problem was a difficult one as it needed someone who had up-to-date ideas yet was willing to relate to the existing cars. At last Godfrey suggested Lord Selsdon should meet his associate from prewar days, Stuart Proctor, who was extremely anxious to get back into the car business from his present post at Boosey and Hawkes, the musical instrument manufacturers. As a result of the meeting, at which Selsdon explained that his and Mathieson's interest in the company was essentially car-related, Proctor suggested various improvements and new ideas and joined the company, first as a fulltime consultant and later as a director.

Proctor was 55 years old and this caused some concern, but against this he had already worked with Godfrey and was known to the senior staff. He was a very capable and competent engineer and made an immediate impact by finalizing the hydraulic brake installation for the existing cars, something which had been experimented upon for some time, as the cable

128

system had, by 1950, become rather archaic. Using mostly Girling parts which were in production for the Austin A70 saloon, he devised a twin-leading-shoe front and single rear action with minimal alterations to the chassis and backplates. The dual master cylinder balance took a little experimenting, but, with a 60/40 front/rear balance, the performance was superb. Hydraulic brakes were fitted to all the WS series cars and were also offered as a conversion for the older cars, the only problem being that the driver had to remember that the handbrake no longer worked on all four wheels!

Proctor also designed a hardtop for the 1500 and around half a dozen were built. Like the bodies themselves, these were ash and aluminium and had to be built to order, no two H.R.Gs having quite the same body dimensions. Whilst his aim was to develop a new H.R.G. Proctor realized that the existing design had to continue until the new one was ready, and

this was proving more difficult than had first been envisaged. In particular, the suppliers of several components had discontinued production and other readily available parts needed extensive modification to suit H.R.G's requirements. For some time he was kept fully occupied updating, modifying and developing the original design.

In the meantime, the cars were still in competitive use, although now right at the end of their international careers. In the *Daily Express* Silverstone Production Car Race in May 1951, Dick Jacobs finally got his TD MG in front of Gerry Ruddock, J.V.S. Brown and Mike Keen in what was to be H.R.G's last major Silverstone appearance. Many of the drivers had moved on, Eric Thompson and Peter Clark to Aston Martin, Ruddock to Lester-MG and Fairman to Jaguar, but there was one major international success to come.

John Gott's much-used JGO 463 had run in the 1948 and 1949 Alpine Rallies in its original Aerodynamic guise, then been rebuilt as a standard two-seater for the 1950 event. In 1951, the 'Old Lady' was entered for her fourth Alpine, supported by Bill Shepherd, whose car was merely on its third time round.

The hydraulic brake conversion. Virtually no alteration to the backplate and twin-leading-shoe assembly at the front was required to accommodate the hydraulic system, left. At the rear the handbrake cables had to be rerouted and now pulled at rightangles to the backplate, above.

A hardtop fitted to the last of the works demonstrators, NPF 206. All the mountings had to be arranged to flex with the body.

John Gott told the story of the event like this: *1951 was to prove a tough year and somehow many prospective entrants must have sensed it for only 66 cars started that year. The emphasis was, however, on quality rather than on quantity for I doubt if such a high-class field has come to the line since. The 1½-litre class, which contained 16 cars, was no exception. There were three Jowett Jupiters: Tommy Wise's was the class-winning record-breaking Le Mans car; Bill Robinson's was the one which had covered itself with glory in the Monte Carlo Rally; and the Frenchman, Armengaud, had just won the Iseran Rally over the Alpine passes. There were six MGs of all types, all competently crewed and prepared. In addition, there were three Simca 'Gran Sport' cars, all driven by experienced French crews. The British contingent was completed by 'Doc' Smallhorn, sportingly driving his special Javelin saloon which he also used on his practice rounds, and Bill Shepherd and ourselves on our veteran H.R.Gs, backed up by a British-crewed Lancia Aurelia.*

As my car had done three Alpines and Bill's had done two, our chances were rather discounted by the experts for it is rare indeed for anyone to subject a car to a second Alpine hammering and a fourth attempt on the same car was regarded as sheer idiocy, but then the experts were not fully aware of the handbuilt workmanship which goes into an H.R.G! Bill and I were bitterly sorry that we could not get a third car to complete a team, but for one reason or another the remainder of the H.R.G. regulars could not get away, and it was left for us to carry the Tolworth banner.

The cars were carefully prepared in view of our past experiences and were identical except for the tyres. I had the earlier 4.75 x 17 wheels and tyres with two spares, whilst Bill had the 5.50 x 16 wheels and tyres with one spare only. The weights were just slightly in my favour and I had the advantage, as I thought, of two spares.

130

In favour of Bill and I was the fact that our previous knowledge of the route gave us a tremendous advantage of knowing when it was essential to hurry and when one could afford to go slow; thus the cars were never driven really hard unless it was absolutely essential to do so.

This year the timed run on the Autostrada had been replaced, much to my relief, by a timed standing kilometre at Monza, whilst there were also timed climbs on the Falzarego and the Stelvio. Fortunately, as it later turned out, the times obtained on these were only for cups and had no bearing on the class final placings. Our high indirect gears were ideal for the timed climbs, but made a fast standing kilometre impossible and Tommy Wise's Jupiter captured this in our class. He was, however, already out of the running as he had lost marks when his electrics failed on the night run.

The run from Bolzano into Cortina was the first real test and Jock Gillespie and I managed it with a reasonable margin. Alas, our jubilation changed to chagrin when Bill's time came up and there was no sign of the black H.R.G. When he did arrive, the front was a little bent: he had had the misfortune to overslide on the loose surface — aptly described as being like ball bearings on ice — and had damaged a wheel, the delay righting it accounting for his lateness.

This left only Bill Robinson's Jupiter and one Simca, plus my H.R.G. 'clean' on our class. Bill Robinson's car was withdrawn when it was found the brake drums were breaking up and the Simca blew up in a cloud of

Two of the Le Mans light-weights were run in the 1952 Nine Hour Race at Goodwood by their new owners, David Blakely and Len Gibbs (National Motor Museum).

Last time of trying. The 1500s of Bill Shepherd, Jack Richmond and Graham Hope-Scott before the start of the Alpine Rally in July, 1952 (Studio Erpe).

sparks just after passing Bill Shepherd on the descent of one of the passes. Jock and I were therefore the only 'clean' car in our class, but we were not without our worries and bothers.

For some unknown reason some foreign body had found its way into the gearbox and tended to jam the gears. Once we got into first gear we stuck there and snap changes were quite impossible. As our whole strategy was based on continual use of bottom and second gears, the cars being geared accordingly, this was a terrific handicap. Not only did it prevent us shining in the timed climbs, but we were terribly slow up-Alp and had to drive dangerously fast downhill to make up for time lost. We had the choice of holding second as long as possible, which was slow out of the corners, or holding bottom all the way up, which was exceedingly slow on the straights. However, we coped.

Quite apart from the gearboxes, we had other worries as well. On one very tight section which only 15 cars completed 'clean', we had a puncture. The wheel was changed in under a minute, which we felt was jet-propelled, and certainly would not have been possible without knock-off hubs and careful planning and practising of movements. Jock and I in a high-speed trial, where such a manoeuvre was compulsory, have changed the front wheels over in 57 seconds, stop to start again, and this proved invaluable in this emergency.

At one petrol pump we took on water in the petrol. This not only entailed feverish work on the pipelines and filters, but also the emptying of almost £3 worth of fuel into the roadway, a procedure which the Italians, who did

132

not know of our plight, thought to be quite crazy. One character indeed returned with a petrol tin, but he was a little late as the flow had then ceased.

Our worst moment was probably in the parc ferme after a night stop. The cars had to be left out in the open all night, irrespective of weather conditions, and packed and started, on the starter, within 5 minutes, or points would be lost. This particular night stop was horribly wet and when it rains in the Alps it makes a real job of it. We rushed out to the car and when I pulled the choke out, the complete wire assembly came away in my hand. The nipple had pulled out and the position of the jets had not altered at all! It would, of course, be easy under normal conditions to lift the bonnet and pull the jets open by hand, but in a parc the bonnet cannot be lifted without penalty. There was only one thing to do and that was to hope the gallant old car would start on the starter without the benefit of choke and after having been left in the open for 23 hours in a mountain downpour. After some heart-stopping moments, she did and what a relief it was to hear the healthy engine beat up once more.

Nancy Mitchell with her 1500 at a Silverstone club meeting in 1952. H.R.Gs remained in competitive use at club level long after they were outclassed in international events.

Gerry Ruddock's lightened and extensively rebuilt Meadows-engined H.R.G. was one of the fastest cars in its class, though, sadly, its original Le Mans body was sacrificed in the process of updating its performance (National Motor Museum).

After this final stroke of misfortune, Lady Luck seemed to smile on us for our 10th flushing of the gearbox seemed to free the gears and, for the last day, which is the hardest of all, we had no trouble at all and the car ran like a dream. Our main worry was tyres for there was no tread left and we had only done 1,650 miles.

Bill Shepherd, meanwhile, had taken over second place and was grimly holding on to it so that he could take over the class lead if we blew up. And so we finished, first and second in the class, the other survivors being two MGs and the gallant Javelin saloon.

The 1951 Alpine was a remarkable British success, with Ian Appleyard (Jaguar XK 120) winning his third Coupe des Alpes and British cars and drivers winning all the classes above 1,100cc. John's Coupe on his fourth drive with the same car is an outstanding record that is likely to endure.

Gott rallied JGO 463 once more, in the 1952 Tulip Rally, where he finished with a clean sheet, but only fourth in the class, thanks to the arrival of the very rapid Porsches just at the start of their competition career. Although the H.R.Gs were no longer competitive, the same could not be said for the drivers. The Alpine story has a postscript in that, when Marcus Chambers returned from overseas, he was invited to become competitions manager for the BMC rally team. Among the first drivers he brought in to what became an all-conquering circus were John Gott,

Nancy Mitchell, Bill Shepherd and Jack Richmond.

Even Peter Clark had his moment of glory in 1951. The single-seater had been rebuilt by Fred Mead and a 1,767cc Lea-Francis engine had been fitted to replace the Standard Vanguard motor. Clark himself was not successful at the wheel but, driven by Joyce Howard, the car took a first, two seconds and a third at the Aston Martin OC Silverstone meeting. At its best, the single-seaater had a maximum speed of nearly 118mph, which must have been rather more than the chassis was ever designed for. Maybe it was understandable that a lady should do well with the car, since the installation of the Lea-Francis unit had resulted in the gearlever being sited frighteningly close to a vital part of Clark's anatomy.

Three 1500s were entered for the 1952 Alpine, driven by Jack Richmond, Bill Shepherd and Graham Hope-Scott. By this time road surfaces were far better and average speeds higher, which meant that the H.R.Gs were well outclassed. Richmond with his new, white 1500 misjudged a corner and

One car which changed its body more than once was HXR 530, originally Jack Scott's Aerodynamic, converted to a lightweight for the 1949 season, and subsequently rebuilt with a full-width body for Bluebelle Gibbs, seen here in action at Silverstone.

retired with damage. On the fourth stage Bill Shepherd went out with gearbox trouble, the source of which was a broken washer (price 4d), leaving Hope-Scott to finish third in the class, albeit having lost a large number of marks in the first two stages.

Throughout the early 1950s, the cars continued to run extensively in all forms of club events, with John Gott, Nancy Mitchell, Jack Richmond and Gerry Ruddock to the fore. Ruddock's Le Mans model H.R.G. had acquired a very light body which, coupled with a deflector-head Meadows engine, made it a very rapid motor car indeed.

Some of the cars remained in the hands of devoted enthusiasts, but many passed with increasing rapidity through more and more impecunious hands, their condition and value depreciating accordingly. Others tried to keep the cars competitive by more or less extreme methods. More powerful engines were installed, lighter bodies and modified suspensions fitted. A case in point was the old green demonstrator, GPE 607, which had been trialled during the 1940s by Alex Francis. He eventually increased the power by fitting a big Mercury engine and

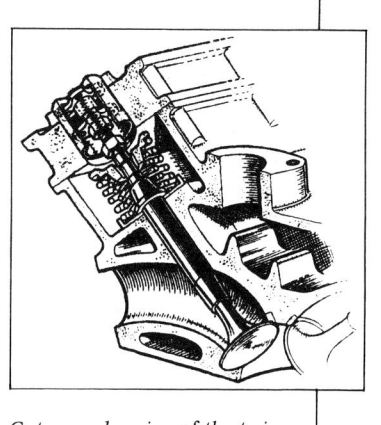

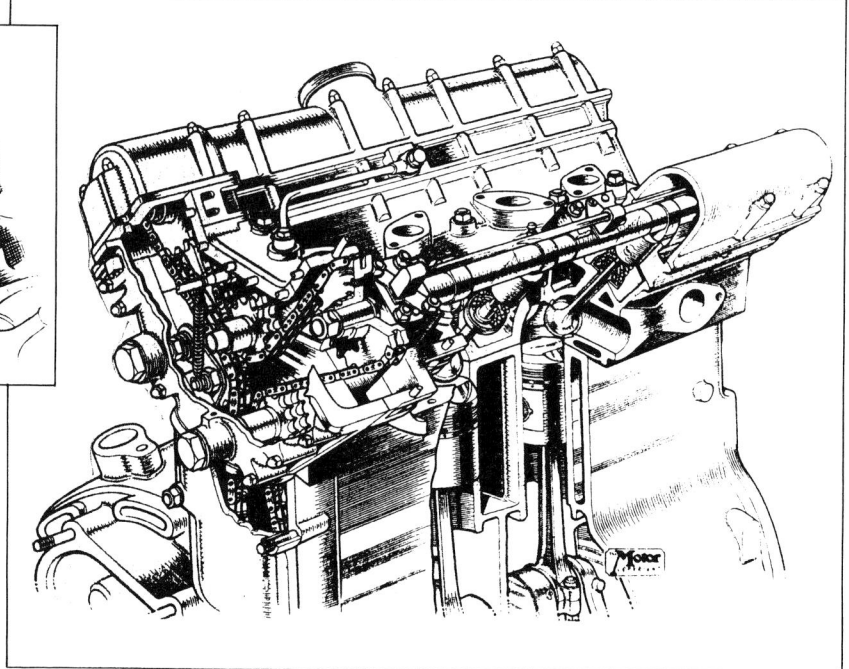

Cutaway drawing of the twin-overhead-camshaft cylinder head designed by Proctor for the long-stroke engine. The detail view of the valve assembly, above, shows the heat dissipating ribs in the water jacket and the threaded adjuster inside the piston-type tappet (The Motor).

The long-stroke twin-cam engine, developed by the factory and used by David Blakely, seen here in process of restoration prior to being reinstalled in HLO 168.

adjusted the bodywork to suit. In the early 1950s the car was dismantled and the original Singer engine and the radiator reappeared in a trials special with Lancia front suspension. Peter Clark's Formula 2 single-seater, with its 1,767cc Lea-Francis engine, was sold to Len Gibbs, who entered it for the 1952 *Daily Express* Trophy race, where it was driven by Michael Keen. It retired in the heats and shortly afterwards it was dismantled and the engine, drive train, petrol tank and H.R.G. hydraulic brakes were installed in a lightweight tubular chassis with all-enveloping body for club racing. Gibbs also bought HXR 530, which his wife Bluebelle raced very competitively in club events for years, and this became highly modified. Following the abandonment of the long-stroke twin-cam head, Gibbs borrowed the casting boxes and built his own version for the car and also added a new body, rather in the style of an AC Ace. The car, in its original form, but with four Amal carburettors, finished 13th overall in the 1952 Goodwood Nine Hour race.

At the factory, Proctor was now ready to make his first major development to improve the performance of the 1500 engine. Although Singers had been producing the SM-series short-stroke block since 1949, it was decided that as an interim measure Proctor should concentrate on the old unit, increasing its power by means of a twin-cam head. 'Proc' was, of course, familiar with the layout, having used it for his earlier aero engine, useful experience since twin-cam four-cylinder heads are not the easiest to make run satisfactorily. It was certainly needed, as times had moved on and the H.R.G. was less and less competitive with the new breed of lightweight sports cars such as the Lester-MGs.

This remarkable silver model of the 1500 was created by Garrards to the order of the Slowak family in Uruguay as a memorial to Robert Slowak who owned chassis number LW139.The replica was scaled from works drawings and measurements taken at the factory.

The head, cast in aluminium, had the four inlet valves on the offside and the exhausts on the nearside. The two camshafts were driven by a chain running over three jockey pulleys. The combustion chambers were hemispherical in concept with 10mm sparking plugs mounted vertically. In May 1953, a press release on the unit was issued, though only one had been built. It was tested in the ex-Peter Clark Le Mans lightweight, which had been sold to David Blakely. Carburation at that time was via twin SUs and trials were also made with Amals, but the project aimed at providing a bolt-on conversion to raise the power of existing engines was discontinued, primarily to switch attention to the new, short-stroke engine. It was a wise decision, because the twin-cam head was set to add some 40-50bhp and the slender, long-stroke rods would never have taken the extra power.

Blakely drove the car with twin-cam engine installed at the Goodwood Nine Hour sports-car race in August 1953. It lapped very quickly, averaging around 77mph, but was beset by a number of minor problems and eventually retired with clutch failure. Later on in the season it raced at both Crystal Palace and Castle Combe, suffering only the inconvenience of a carburettor casting failure.

138

Had Giuseppi Verdi been alive, HLO 168 would have undoubtedly played an operatic role in the tragedy that he surely would have written about Blakely's subsequent history. Blakely, the stepson of Humphrey Cook of ERA fame, was a talented driver and a well-known young man about town. Following the initial experiments with the twin-cam, he persuaded the company to lend him the updated version of the engine and this was installed, not in the original HLO 168, but in a new car altogether (carrying the same registration), which had been designed and built by Blakely and Anthony Findlater. The car was called the Emperor and the aim was to go into production with it.

The idea was doomed to failure — there was no finance for a start — but the car, described as the 'Emperor-H.R.G', was completed and raced at the 1954 Brands Hatch Boxing Day meeting, where it finished second in the Kent Cup. Its outward appearance was reminiscent of the Sopwith Armstrong-Siddelely Sphinx and it was built round a square-tube chassis, Volkswagen front suspension and a De Dion rear arrangement.

Whilst Blakely's racing ability was considerable — he was nominated for the 1955 Bristol works team for Le Mans — his business acumen was somewhat less and his private life was, of its time, sensational, centring round a stormy relationship with a blonde nightclub hostess by the name of Ruth Ellis. In the spring of 1955 the affair was drawing to a close. The Emperor was entered for the British Empire Trophy at Oulton Park, but blew up in practice and could not be repaired in time for the Goodwood Easter Monday meeting. On Easter Sunday, Ellis shot Blakely: she was subsequently convicted of murder and became the last woman in England to be hanged.

As the Blakely tragedy was being played out, development work on the new model continued at the works and production of the old-style cars dwindled away. The short-stroke Singer SM engine had now completely superseded the long-stroke type, but orders for the 1500 had almost come to an end. The final batch of 12 cars was sold to the USA through the good offices of Jack Wherry of International Motors, Maquoketa, Iowa. Jack put in an enormous amount of work on behalf of H.R.Gs in the States, forming an Owners' Club, carrying stocks of spares and radiating enthusiasm. These last cars, the WS series, were fitted with the short-stroke engines and hydraulic brakes and were arguably the best H.R.Gs ever made. They were, however, by nature of a stopgap pending the arrival of the new car and as early as 1953 rumours of its production were starting to circulate. Apart from revealing something of the engine development, the works stayed silent on the subject. But the time had come for something new, and the arrival of the long-awaited model was keenly anticipated.

The twin-cam

10

1955-1956

In February 1955 the long-awaited new H.R.G. was announced. The development of the Mark II had started with the arrival of Stuart Proctor, and the engine, not unnaturally, stemmed from his initial work improving the performance of the long-stroke Singer. The new car was really new: the only items in its construction already in use were the engine block, a few instruments, the steering wheel and the radiator badge. Even the steering wheel and most of the instruments were changed shortly afterwards.

The chassis consisted of twin, parallel $3\frac{3}{4}$ in diameter 16swg tubes, with a slight upward curve forward of the cockpit. The chassis had three tubular crossmembers, plus two hoop-like bridges at the rear on which the rear suspension was mounted. The wheelbase was 8ft with a 4ft track. The front suspension was independent, with wishbones on top and a lower transverse spring consisting of three 5in wide leaves. Woodhead Monroe telescopic shock absorbers were used, together with coil springs, whose setting could be varied. At the rear, the arrangement was reversed, with the transverse spring located on top of the hooped crossmembers and the wishbones operating underneath.

The wheel spokes were cast from very light magnesium alloy and consisted of six-point spiders on which the 4in rims carrying 16 x 5.25 tyres were attached. The design was novel in that the wheel studs extended behind the spiders to locate the $10\frac{5}{8}$ in diameter steel brake discs. The new

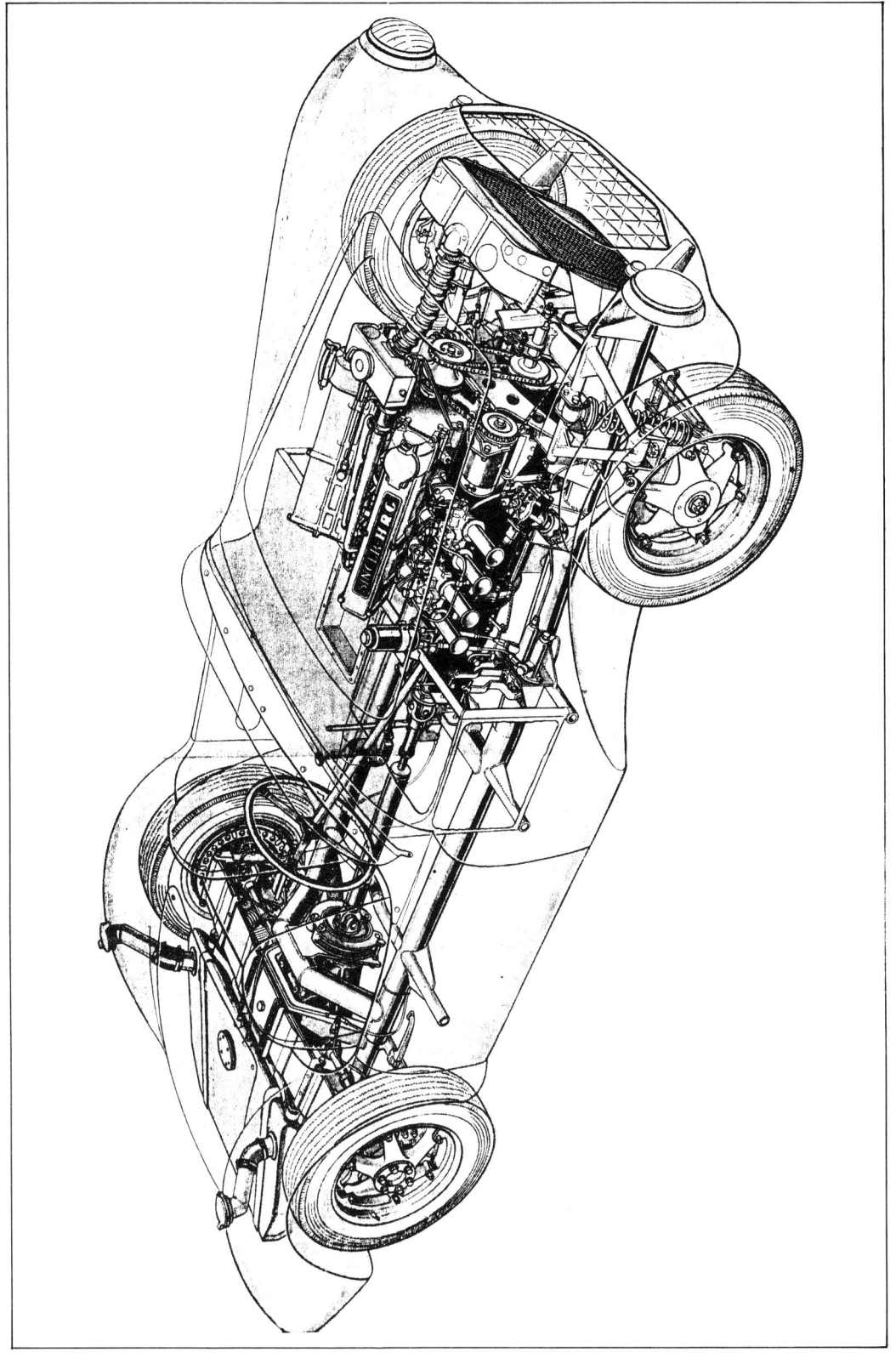

The prototype twin-cam as depicted in cutaway form by The Autocar in February, 1955. The salient features of the twin-tube chassis, with independent suspension all round, are clearly visible.

The first H.R.G. Mark II, the prototype twin-cam, outside the front of the Oakcroft Road factory in February, 1955.

H.R.G. was only the second British sports car to feature disc brakes: unlike Jaguar with its Dunlop system, H.R.G. manufactured a modification of the Palmer aircraft design. This operated by means of synthetic rubber bags which, when pressurized, expanded against kidney-shaped disc pads, forcing them against the disc. A protective layer was necessary to prevent the rubber from being melted by the heat build-up. The hydraulic system was by Lockheed. Special spring-loaded pads were fitted on the spider extensions to eliminate disc rattle. Each ring-shaped disc was attached by its outer edge to the wheel spider. Consequently, the calipers fitted inside the ring, not in the more conventional position outside a centrally mounted disc. The combination of magnesium alloy wheels and the disc brakes was calculated to save over 50lb of unsprung weight and it was claimed that each set of pads could be stripped and replaced within 10 minutes. H.R.G. also supplied the Palmer unit for use on the Mark IX Cooper 500, but whereas the Coopers were fitted with two pads on the rear only, the H.R.Gs had three pads on each front brake as well.

Steering was effected initially by one of the old four-spoke Dover wheels, but subsequently by a wood-rimmed alloy steering wheel, operating through a Burman recirculating-ball steering box, modified from Singer use. This was fitted on the offside chassis tube and operated via a horizontal arm and linkage to a slave arm mounted on the rear of the front crossmember, connected to the wheels by a split track rod. The steering ratio was $1\frac{3}{4}$ turns, lock to lock.

Into this chassis was fitted the latest development of the twin-cam, 73mm x 89.6mm Singer-based engine. Stuart Proctor had gone a long way towards resolving the various problems of the twin-cam. Compression

143

ratio, using domed and scalloped Martlett pistons, was 8.8:1, with 10mm KLG T240 plugs set almost vertically between the cams. The effect of the RR 50 alloy head was to raise the power output of the engine from around 55bhp in its Singer form to nearly 110bhp. This necessitated the installation of a forged Laystall crankshaft and additional strengthening to other components, including the clutch and gearbox housings. As announced, the twin-cam engine could be fitted with 40mm horizontal, twin-choke Solex carburettors, or $1\frac{1}{2}$in SUs. As with the earlier, experimental heads, the exhaust valve guides were water cooled. The $1\frac{1}{2}$in exhaust and $1^{11}/_{16}$in inlet valves were operated directly by the camshafts with piston-type tappets fitted to absorb the sideways force of the cam lobes. Exhaust was by means of a four-branch manifold sweeping outwards, clear of the chassis, with carefully devised balancing between inner and outer pipes. Cooling was provided for by the Singer water pump mounted on the front of the block and a Singer radiator set at a raked angle

Three-quarter rear view of the prototype, showing the dashboard layout including the 'old' instruments and steering wheel.

ahead of the front crossmember. This was supplemented by a small header tank in front of the cam boxes, and there was a belt-driven fan mounted independently on the crossmember.

The strengthened Singer gearbox gave overall ratios of 4:1 (top), 5:1 (third), 7.34:1 (second) and 12.27:1 (first and reverse). At the rear of the propeller shaft a mechanically-operated parking brake was fitted, connecting to the handbrake. Behind this was the Salisbury hypoid-bevel differential and the drive shafts. A horizontal, 12-gallon fuel tank with twin fillers was mounted on tubes welded to the rear end of the chassis, feeding the carburettors via twin electric pumps.

The prototype aluminium body was built by Wakefields of East Molesey and, with 7in ground clearance, it looked somewhat gawky despite its attractively swept lines. Accessibility, however, was excellent: the entire front body section was hinged at the front and could be lifted clear of the engine bay, in addition to the usual bonnet panel. The radiator grille was cut out in the octagonal shape of the trademark. Car and body complete weighed approximately 1,600lb dry and a provisional price in the £1,700 bracket was announced.

The prototype, registered VPH 188, was tested extensively and the second car, registered XPL 178, was completed in August 1955 for David Calvert. The bodywork of this second example was lowered and more rounded with various detail improvements. At the time, a number of alternative ideas were in mind, including the production of a 2/4-seater coupe. The styling sketches have not survived but contemporary reports referred to them as being in keeping with the latest Italian design.

A short-chassis, 7ft 6in wheelbase car was undertaken for a customer who had established himself as a promising racing driver. Unfortunately, his position in relation to a family trust concerned with a major public company was such that his premature demise through, for example, motor sport might have had serious commercial repercussions. Accordingly, on

The prototype twin-cam chassis reveals its general layout. Unusual details are the coils supplementing the transverse leaf springs and the transmission brake ahead of the final drive unit.

Close-up of the twin-cam's front suspension shows the wishbone and spring arrangement as well as the twin caliper operating inside the brake disc which is located on self-adjusting studs.

Twin-cam rear suspension, with the leaf spring on top and the wishbone underneath, the reverse of the front arrangement. A sliding splined joint accommodates changes in drive shaft length.

hearing of his proposed purchase, his legal advisers applied pressure, H.R.G. were paid for the work they had done and the chassis, engine and running gear were dismantled. Many years later, the components were obtained and reassembled by John Peet. The fourth car, 15 APB, was built to the order of Paul Fletcher and this represents the most advanced development of the type, the lines becoming more stylish and the fittings more refined. A fifth chassis frame was constructed, but not built up into a car.

From an early stage, the twin-cam project had been developed in close co-operation with Singer Motors Ltd. The H.R.G. concept was entirely

sporting and production numbers were envisaged to be small. However, the board of Singer Motors were interested by Stuart Proctor's ideas, which they saw as providing a possible answer to the flagging fortunes of their company. The Singer Hunter saloon (which used the block fitted in the twin-cam), was not selling well and the 'sports' Singer SM roadster hardly at all. Proctor enthusiastically developed the proposition that Singers should build the chassis and bodies of the new H.R.G, producing it in quantity as a Singer. A. E. Hunt, the managing director of Singer Motors, took note of the idea, but was in no way disposed to countenance the

The body of the last of the twin-cams, with its lower, smoother contours and extended nose, shows the development which had taken place since the construction of the first car.

From the front, the last twin-cam looks purposeful and uncluttered. Twin streamlined blisters replace the large central bonnet bulge. The split windscreen is easily removable for racing.

Comparison of VPH 188 and 15 APB shows how much progress the body design had made towards a production-car level of refinement. The boot space is largely occupied by the petrol tank, with its central filler, leaving room for perhaps just a little more than the proverbial toothbrush.

thought until the H.R.G. had proved itself. A second proposal, that the twin-cam engine should be dropped into the existing Hunter saloon to revitalize it, was also made and, in view of the ominously rising overdraft, the Singer board elected to take this somewhat less expensive option.

In October 1955, the Singer Hunter 75 was announced, the '75' representing its power output. The model was a standard Hunter with a detuned, production version of the twin-cam head. This was made of chrome iron, as opposed to the H.R.G. head, which was alloy, and whereas the H.R.G. manifolding was of the crossflow pattern, on the Singer two Solex 32 PB10-2 carburettors were mounted vertically, directly over the inlet valves. There were various dimensional changes too: for example, the exhaust valves were reduced to 1⅜in diameter and the compression ratio

lowered to 8:1. These changes, and a very 'unflowed' exhaust manifold, brought the power down, but 75bhp at 5,250rpm was still very respectable. Conventional 14mm Champion L10S sparking plugs were fitted.

But it was all too little and too late. The Singer Hunter 75 appeared at the Earls Court Motor Show and some 20 engines appear to have been built. One Hunter 75 was driven regularly by Leo Shorter, Singer's technical director, but in November 1955, with a bank overdraft now approaching £500,000, the directors accepted a bid from the Rootes Group and by January 1956 the takeover was complete. One of Sir William Rootes' first acts was to abandon the Hunter 75 and the project was quite literally junked. What happened to the engines is a mystery: rumour has it they were fitted in the next convenient batch of saloons and sold off.

Until the Rootes takeover was announced, H.R.G. were unaware of the

In addition to the opening bonnet, the entire front end could be hinged up for easy access to the engine. This is 15 APB again, showing its twin SU carburettors.

The head of the twin-cam engine, seen from underneath, reveals its hemispherical combustion chambers and generous ports.

The Calvert/Green twin-cam in action during the Goodwood Nine Hour Race in August, 1955, prior to the excursion into the turnip field (C. Dunn).

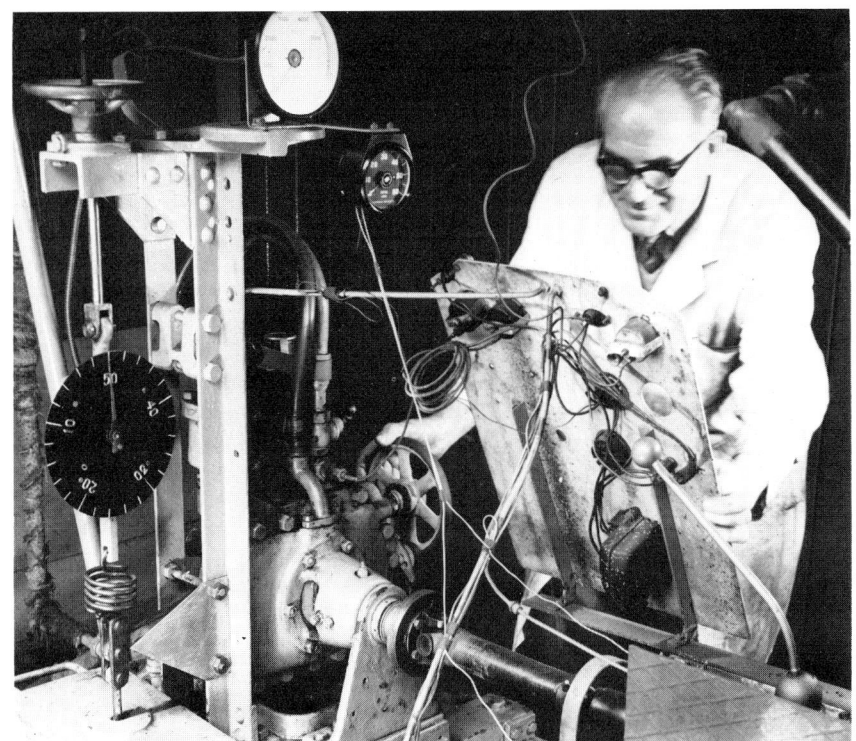

Much of the development of the twin-cam engine was monitored on the factory dynamometer. Here, David Eadington is at the controls.

true state of Singer's finances. Overnight, the major expansion they had so nearly obtained had disappeared. Worse still, it became apparent very rapidly that the source of engine blocks and components was also going to dry up as Rootes embarked on a policy of badge-engineering — from now on, Singers would be merely re-labelled Hillmans. Discussions with the new Rootes-Singer board foundered — yes, they would continue to produce blocks for H.R.G: how many thousand would be ordered? The directors of H.R.G. Engineering Co Ltd, having invested so much time and money in the development of the twin-cam project, decided to call it a day and on July 13, 1956 the last Singer-engined H.R.G, a standard sports two-seater for an American customer, left the works. It can have been only small consolation that in the year ending July 31, 1956 the new Rootes-Singer organization recorded a loss of over £600,000.

Stuart Proctor was fond of quoting the Scriptures and the words of the hymn 'God moves in a mysterious way' were particularly apt. But for intervention by Rootes, Singer would have fallen flat on its face and would undoubtedly have taken H.R.G. with it. However, even if some other answer had been found, by some miracle, the question arises whether the twin-cam would ever have made it anyway. Various forecasts were made for possible production: 12 in 1955, possibly 25 in 1956. It was aimed at a very small slice of the market and history records that the market itself was changing. By the 1956 Motor Show, Frazer-Nash were exhibiting their last model, the Continental, Allard their Palm Beach. It was the end of an era and the beginning of a new one. On the next stand to Frazer-Nash, Colin Chapman was showing the ultra-light Lotus 11 Le Mans, the shape of things to come in the world of competition sports car. Also at the exhibition were displays of MGAs, TR3s and Austin-Healey 100s:

between mass production and ultra-high performance, there was very little room for the producers of low-production, handbuilt sports cars for road use.

The twin-cam had a brief competition history. Its only major appearance was at the Goodwood Nine Hour race on Saturday, August 20, 1955. The entry, as usual, was a private one, by David Calvert, with Richard Green as his co-driver, in a class including entries from Connaught, Cooper, Lotus and a Porsche driven by Stirling Moss. XPL 178, the second twin-cam, was completed a week before the race so that practice was a mixture of getting to know the car and trying to run it in. During the Thursday night practice, engine trouble was detected and traced to a broken piston circlip, which had caused extensive damage. On Friday morning Doug Orchard set to and, by that evening, had rebuilt the engine completely, installing loose-fitting pistons and bearings in an attempt to compensate for the lack of running in. Despite this, the engine needed some hours running and, as the works personnel were almost exhausted and were vitally needed for the next racing day, Lord Selsdon stepped forward and put mileage on the clock by driving the car through the night backwards and forwards between Tolworth and Portsmouth. More than a little anxiety was felt when the factory opened on Saturday morning without any sign of Lord Selsdon or the car, but he arrived shortly afterwards and all was well.

In the race, the car ran very reliably for four hours, but around dusk, Calvert had an excursion into the infield and contrived to blank off the radiator with turnip leaves. This resulted in repeated visits to the pits over a two-hour period, during which time both the radiator and water pump were replaced very rapidly indeed. Despite ominous noises from the gearbox, the car ran regularly for the last part of the race, finishing seventh in the 1½-litre class at 53mph behind the class-winning Connaught of Leston and Scott-Brown, who averaged 77mph. But for the turnips, the difference would have been very much less. The race was marred by the death of the erstwhile H.R.G. driver Mike Keen, who was killed in an accident involving his Cooper-Bristol.

Two twin-cams in the hands of David Calvert and Paul Fletcher took part in the *Autosport* Championship race for production sports cars at the 1956 Goodwood Easter meeting, with Calvert finishing fourth in XPL 178 and Fletcher retiring with 15 APB. XPL 178 ran in a few more meetings and finally disappeared to the West Country from where it was later rescued by Brian Symes. 15 APB was purchased by Hartwells, who sold Rootes products, but its history is uncertain until, in the early 1960s, it was sold to America. In the early 1970s, it was brought by the Pennsylvania H.R.G. enthusiast, Gary Ford, who set about tuning the engine, then in dire need of attention. In 1975, the author drove 15 APB for Gary at the US Grand Prix meeting at Watkins Glen, being the second 1½-litre car to finish in the historic race. The car, with tappets set at 40 thou clearance, had a remarkable turn of speed, with a surge of power coming in just below 4,000rpm. Its roadholding was impeccable.

What if the twin-cam had appeared a decade earlier? Bar the disc brakes, it might have done — but then life is full of 'ifs'.....

The end of the line   **11**

1957-1966

The decision to end car production gave Stuart Proctor the chance to pursue other ideas. On joining the company, he had expressed the opinion that there was a large and profitable market for 'bolt-on goodies', improvements for mass-produced cars, but all his efforts had been directed to the new car development and, apart from keeping his interest in the accessory market, nothing had been finalized. Now he turned his attention to this area of design and the H.R.G. crossflow head for the 1,500cc B-series BMC engine was produced. This engine was then in use in the MGA, Riley 1.5, MG Magnette and Wolseley 1500 cars as well as the more prosaic Austins and Morrises. The head was cast in alloy, with twin SUs on the offside and a four-branch exhaust manifold on the nearside. The unit was offered as a package, complete with competition pistons, special rocker cover and cold air box. MGA valves were used and alternative $1\frac{1}{2}$in or $1\frac{3}{4}$in carburettors could be fitted.

The performance of the head was excellent and the works issued the comparative figures in the accompanying table, showing that an H.R.G-equipped MGA could outperform the factory Twin-Cam version on all points. The maximum power output claimed for an engine with the H.R.G. head was around 125bhp and could be boosted to 150bhp by fitting Weber twin-choke carburettors. The head itself was priced at £58 10s 0d and, assembled with valves and springs, £68 10s 0d.

	MGA coupe	MGA with H.R.G. head	MGA Twin-Cam
Acceleration:			
20-40mph in top gear	13.6sec	8.9sec	10.7sec
60-80mph in top gear	17.6sec	11.9sec	13.9sec
10-30mph in third gear	8.1sec	6.7sec	8.3sec
20-40mph in third gear	7.9sec	6.0sec	6.5sec
Maximile speed:			
Timed $\frac{3}{4}$ mile after 1 mile accelerating from rest	92.0mph	102.3mph	101.3mph
Fuel consumption:			
At steady 50mph	43.2mpg	44.5mpg	33.5mpg
At steady 90mph	24.8mpg	25.0mpg	22.0mpg

Proctor's designs also included plug holders and plug spanners, similar to those fitted to the H.R.G. cars, air intakes for carburettors and a range of aluminium rocker covers suitable for BMC engines, both A-series and B-series, as well as Fords and Standard-Triumphs. They were very good looking, available with either black or polished finish, and retailed at between £4 and £6.

Another production item was the exhaust extractor, also marketed by Alexander Engineering. This device consisted of an attachment to the end of the exhaust pipe, aimed at improving gas flow. It was claimed that it increased efficiency and improved fuel consumption because it incorporated a reverse-wave trap, that it was light in weight with no moving parts and, for good measure, gave a smoother exhaust note — all for 50 shillings!

Components of the H.R.G. crossflow cylinder head conversion for the 1,500cc B-series BMC engine.

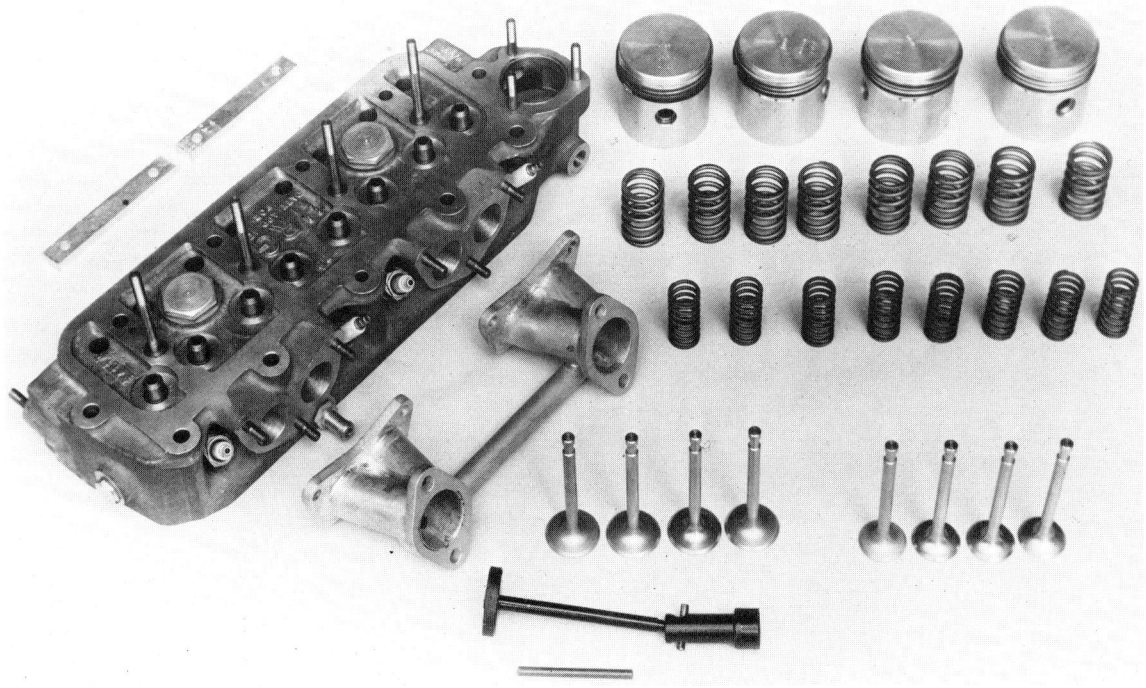

A result of producing these accessories was an approach from V. W. Derrington, who had taken over the patterns and tools of the Alta OHV head for the Series MM Morris Minor from Geoffrey Taylor when he retired, and suggested that H.R.G. should also produce that conversion. Although the market was almost exhausted, a few batches were produced and sold. The B-series head was, however, extremely successful, both performance-wise and financially. On one occasion a professional financial adviser recommended to the H.R.G. board that if 400 heads per week were produced, all the worries of the company would be over! This was too much for Proctor, who thought of himself as a designer, not a commercial businessman: even he could not imagine where that number of sales would come from! Nevertheless, this specialized design market continued to interest the company and Proctor turned his attention to the new Ford 105E engine, developing two options. The first was a 'quickie' conversion to improve performance by means of an improved manifold and twin carburettors. The second was the design of an overhead-cam

Overhead view of the engine compartment of an MGA equipped with the H.R.G. crossflow cylinder head.

The VX at an Association meeting, its lines and proportions creating an impression of enormous length. Doug Orchard, second from left, looks quizzical.

head, offering serious prospects of major power improvement.

The success of these conversions contributed considerably to the volume of business of the company. By 1962 it was decided to look into the possibility of a new car, built up round an H.R.G-converted Ford engine and parts, and in 1963 a new tubular spaceframe was designed to take the engine. It had a wheelbase of 7ft 6in, a track of 4ft 2in, an overall length of 12ft and a ground clearance of 6in. The front suspension was independent, with coil springs, telescopic shock absorbers, Girling disc brakes, unequal-length wishbones and an anti-roll bar. The rear suspension was standard Ford Cortina with drum brakes. There were dual master cylinders. The steering was rack-and-pinion, $2\frac{1}{2}$ turns, lock to lock.

In 1964 the car was running in chassis form and serious consideration was given to production, but it was thought that Ford parts were readily available for many 'specials' and other component cars already available on the market. It would be better if the company obtained the co-operation of one of the mass-producers not in the sports or 'specials' area. A former owner of an H.R.G, Stan Tett, was able to introduce the company to Vauxhall Motors, and in due course a meeting was arranged between their managing director, Proctor and Grace Leather.

After a lengthy discussion, when it was made clear that Vauxhall Motors had no intention of actively supporting competition work, it was also indicated that they would assist as far as possible with the supply of information and favourable terms for parts. If the final outcome were successful then future production could be discussed. In the meantime,

Cockpit of the VX. The driving position and handling were up to the best H.R.G. standards, but the internal finish could undoubtedly have been improved given more time.

Vauxhall would not consider any other similar approaches. Consequently, the Ford project was abandoned, the engine and gearbox being lifted out and sold to David Daniel, the owner of a particularly beautiful 1500 in California, who installed them in his car for general use, keeping the original motor for high days and holidays. When the Oakcroft Road factory was cleared out in 1966, the Ford chassis was sold off to a Mr Shepherd, who built it up into a car. In 1969 it surfaced briefly less engine and with very substantial chassis damage.

The Vauxhall-based design got underway in 1964 and the strategy was in essence similar to the twin-cam plan. H.R.G. would develop the car and produce a limited number, during which time, hopefully, it would be adapted by Vauxhall for the mass market, possibly with a glass-fibre body. The basis was the VX 4/90 1,600cc engine and, as with the Ford project, as many standard Vauxhall components as possible would be incorporated. Unlike the twin-cam, the new design relied heavily on components already available and increased power was obtained by the traditional technique of improving the breathing of the original head, plus a competition camshaft. The body was carried on a square-tube framework and, once again, was fabricated by Wakefields at East Molesey. The coachworks did a fine job technically, but aesthetically the design left something to be desired: forward of the windscreen the bonnet was reminiscent of a Jaguar E; to the rear of the cockpit the style became Lotus Elan or Ferrari. However, the two were linked by a wide door which had the effect of making the car appear far longer than it was and this was exaggerated by the use of small, 13in wheels. One reason for this long centre section lay in the fact that Proctor was a tall man and suffered from a stiff leg, so the design suited him well.

Behind the boarded-off section of the rear workshop the new car was completed with a minimum of publicity, interested parties being kept at bay by a large notice proclaiming 'KEEP OUT, THIS ANIMAL BITES' in the fitting shop. The construction was not without its headaches over the supply of Vauxhall parts, the main problem being that Vauxhall had recently computerized their stores and paperwork procedure. It often seemed that it might be quicker to make the parts rather than wait for their arrival with no certainty then that they were what was ordered. These problems were mainly overcome by purchasing from a local Vauxhall agent, albeit at normal trade prices.

Whilst this new development was taking place, general engineering continued to flourish and a great deal of goodwill was built up with diverse production including mechanical equipment for X-ray mountings, both medical and industrial, as well as pulverized fuel samplers for the CEGB and products for the mechanical handling market. A large number of trays designed to hold rat bait were made to the specification of the Ministry of Agriculture and Fisheries, and following the arrival of coypus in East Anglia a mark II design, of increased capacity, had to be introduced. In addition, an increasing amount of machining and subassembly work for the Cooper and Brabham companies was going on. But the decision to go back to car development provided a renewed interest to all at the factory.

Engine compartment of the VX, showing the Vauxhall power unit, square-tube frame, header tank, and air intake trunking for the twin SU carburettors.

158

Throughout the design and development of the VX project, Lord Selsdon had taken a considerable interest, but his unexpected death at sea in 1964 created a series of new worries. T.A.S.O. Mathieson had gone to live in Portugal, having appointed a friend in the financial world as alternate director, and although Lord Selsdon's son Malcolm joined the board, his interest was mainly in sports cars in a general way and in following up his father's interest. As the months went by, it was obvious that the executors of the late Lord Selsdon wished to realize his investment in the company and Mathieson thought that, if he did the same, it could simplify any possible restructuring, as he was no longer able to take an active interest.

During the following months, while efforts were made to raise the necessary replacement capital, the VX was progressing and at the beginning of 1966 it was considered complete, albeit with one or two odd features, including what looked suspiciously like a Victor rear window as the windscreen. The cockpit was trimmed with some rather nasty quilted fabric and several details were unfinished. It was not officially road-tested and its performance was never properly assessed. However, those who drove it hard claimed it was akin to the highly-regarded Lotus Elan. Like all prototypes, it had its teething problems, the high-lift cam proving too savage for the drive gears.

Grace Leather with her 1500, the car originally driven by Jack Richmond on the 1952 Alpine Rally.

It soon became apparent to the directors that replacement capital was not forthcoming. While approaches to various companies connected with the motor trade or motor racing could be followed up, it was obvious that the assets of the company were all important in such negotiations and its style of business, including the relationship with its staff, car owners and customers, was of little importance, so that any commitments on the maintenance of goodwill given on takeover would not be binding in any way. This situation was totally unacceptable to the people involved, and at the beginning of 1966 it was decided to look into the question of voluntary liquidation, bearing in mind all the factors by then affecting the company.

H. R. Godfrey, having retired some years previously, was now in poor health, unable to walk and, although interested in the company, could not attend meetings or assist in any way. David Eadington was approaching 60 and was gradually working towards retirement, intending to return to his home in Northumberland. Stuart Proctor, although 70, still wished to continue in fulltime employment, but at that age it was considered it would be difficult to safeguard his job. Grace Leather was not in good health and wanted to retire. At a meeting in January 1966, Grace Leather was instructed to prepare the figures for a voluntary liquidation: on April 4, 1966, an extraordinary meeting of the shareholders was held and Mr Peter Hale was appointed liquidator.

Even before the April meeting, Proctor had been offered employment by V. W. Derrington and, due to his personal circumstances, felt that he must accept and did so. The decision to liquidate came as no shock to the

160

employees and, with the assurance that everyone would be helped to find alternative employment, the liquidation took place smoothly. The liquidator took the view that it would be in the interest of everyone to carry on trading so that all subcontract and general engineering orders could be completed, the plant and equipment sold to the best advantage and the employees satisfactorily settled in new employment. Eadington and Grace Leather were given the opportunity to resolve these various matters and close the factory down in a manner that reflected their own and the integrity of the company over the previous 30 years.

The workforce had dwindled to about 10. Fred Mead had died, having left some years earlier with ill health. Doug Orchard had left to join Vanwall after the decision to cease car production in 1955. Although starting as a general fitter/mechanic, he showed a particular flair for engine fitting and tuning, so when he was offered a job with Vanwall at the height of their success it was obvious he would take it; Dickie Watson, who had assisted Doug on the twin-cam project, went with him. Bill Constable, who had come with Mead and Orchard from AFN, was still with the firm at the closure, but went straight to other employment, as did Harry Edwards, an ex-apprentice who became the engine fitter. Ron Couzens and Brian Denham, both of whom had served their apprenticeships at Tolworth, went to the Brabham organization, at Byfleet, together with many of the machine tools and other equipment. In addition to their statutory redundancy payments all were given lump sums commensurate with their jobs and length of service. This, at a time when such payments to shop-floor employees were not usual, made the break a little more bearable.

In April 1966 a statement was put out by the company to the car owners

Brian Symes continued Nancy Mitchell's successful competition career with NPC 532 and is seen here on his way to a premier award in the 1964 Exeter Trial. Note the flexible rubber strip rear wings (National Motor Museum/ Michael Ware).

and customers advising them of the liquidation as follows: *The decision has been taken after many months of consideration and many factors have been taken into account, including the difficulty of obtaining suitable skilled labour, the age and health of various members of the Board and Management, and the fact that the general economic conditions prevailing in the country today do not help a small business with limited financial resouces in the face of competition from larger organizations.*

It was therefore felt that this step was the only one to take in the interests of all closely associated with the company. By taking this step we are able to determine as far as possible the future position of such items as the supply of spares for H.R.G. cars which is, I am sure, of paramount importance to all owning cars and I am very pleased to be able to tell you that Mr Roberts, who, as you know, has owned an H.R.G. for many years and is a director of Trident Garages Limited, has arranged for Trident Garages (Ripley) Limited, of High Street, Ripley, to take over the spares for H.R.G. cars.

The last car in for repair, appropriately the works demonstrator MPG 177, which had done so much for the marque in competitions, left the factory at the end of April 1966 and closure commenced. As announced, the car spares, drawings and jigs went to Trident Garages, who also purchased the VX.

The premises, which had been purchased by the company from Godfrey in 1963, were sold to the adjoining cosmetic manufacturers, who demolished them to expand their own factory buildings. It was a sad but inevitable end to the H.R.G. Engineering Company Limited, the only consolation being that the shareholders did decide their own destiny and, financially, the outcome was satisfactory. It had to end and it could not have done so in a nicer way.

Epilogue

The H.R.G. Association

H.R.G. ladies are a tough breed. Ann Dussek does her best to improve traction whilst avoiding an impromptu mud-pack from the front wheels of LHT 670 (National Motor Museum/Michael Ware).

In 1960, a group of younger H.R.G. owners got together to form a club. The proposal met with some reservation from the company and some of the older owners, who regarded Oakcroft Road as a club in its own right. Nonetheless, the idea went ahead — but the 'club' became an Association and H.R. Godfrey was invited to become Patron, rather than Chairman or President. In the best H.R.G. traditions, things were going to be different.

From the start the Association, under the secretaryship of the author, developed in a curious but single-minded manner. There were no written rules, but the Association was to be run by owners for owners with welcome support from company personnel and notable ex-owners. (What constituted a notable ex-owner was never precisely defined). Despite the occasional gaffe, the Association attempted to maintain a separate identity, but also a close relationship with the factory, and this understanding was reciprocated when the directors presented the

Association with a silver salver for annual competition, which became the Association's premier award. Other forms of competition were encouraged by gifts of trophies from Guy Robins, John Gott, John Newton, Ted Dennis and Charles Meisl. These did much to bring cars out into various forms of competitive activity and helped to boost their prestige and encourage their maintenance in good condition.

During the 1960s, the Association promoted a number of events and the H.R.G's dominance of production car trials, notably in the hands of Ted Dennis, Brian Symes and Roger Williams, was such that stickers started appearing on other competitors' cars reading 'Help stamp out H.R.Gs'. At one time regulations for trials started appearing with the H.R.G. listed as a trials special, something which was fought tooth and nail. Somehow the factory kept finding enough spare parts to keep the cars running, but a number of techniques were devised to reduce trials damage, such as flexible wings, raised silencer systems and the use of steel deflector plates in front of the sump and exhaust system. In the events themselves, various adjustments were made to the cars to minimize errors, such as locking fuel systems on and preventing gearlevers from slipping out of first gear under load. The use of especially suitable tyres with heavy sidewalls became common, resulting in a long string of successes.

Richard Clark has won the Association's premier award no less than eight times with the 1½-litre originally owned by Elsie Redfern. After over 45 years it is still a formidable performer (Neill Bruce).

The start of an H.R.G. versus MG race at Silverstone in 1964. The author is on pole position with LHT 670 and behind are the 1500s of John Peet and Adrien Sturgeon. Further back are the Keith Williams 1100, two more 1500s and an Aerodynamic (National Motor Museum/Michael Ware).

In co-operation with the MG Car Club, a series of H.R.G. versus TC and TD races were held at Silverstone and the Association also assisted in the foundation of the Historic Sports Car Club. The difficulty of this type of racing was that the H.R.G, whilst historically very successful, obtained its results through reliability rather than outright speed, so that by the early 1950s it was uncompetitive. The MG, on the other hand, was progressively developed for racing and had sufficient 'meat' in its basic block to allow extensive development so that many of the old T-series cars were able to circulate considerably faster than when they first left Abingdon.

The activities of the Association were treated with generally amused tolerance by the company (interposed with the occasional 'rocket' to the effect that the firm was not operating entirely for the personal convenience of young men with old cars), but when the factory closed, the Association took on an increasing importance, co-incidentally at a time when the price of the cars, which had sunk to £200 or less, had started to rise again, bringing with it a new breed of owner, the investor.

After working closely with Tridents for two years, the Association was asked to take over the stock of spares, which it did in 1968, and was able to store them thanks to the kindness of Adrien Sturgeon and later, Alan Dussek. For the next eight years, Alan Dussek cleaned, greased, catalogued and despatched parts all over the world, to establish a club reputation second to none. Under Ian Mahany's direction, many new parts were manufactured and original patterns improved.Long-forgotten stocks were tracked down and owners have since been able to enjoy a spares service which is as near as can be today to that found at the factory. On the death of Alan Dussek, the parts were stored first by Charles Meisl

Jo Bonnier at the beginning of his racing career, driving an H.R.G. in 1953. He bought the car secondhand in 1951, partly because 'it looked just like a proper competition car should look'.

Left: the ex-Bonnier car as found in a wood in Sweden. Right: Roger Ericson's rebuild of the car in progress. The ash body frame was reconstructed from original timbers and new parts made to factory drawings.

Roger Ericson's rebuild well advanced. A new radiator was constructed entirely from scratch.

and then at Ian Mahany's garage at Harpenden, where an H.R.G. repair service is also carried out.

After 50 years, a very high proportion of all the H.R.Gs built have survived and most are carefully preserved in their original condition. The Association has maintained a policy of originality wherever possible and has set its face against the production of 'clones' and 'replicas' or the exhumation of vehicular corpses.

Sadly, today these beautiful cars are seldom if ever seen. There is now no 'competition slot' for the H.R.G. other than for a handful of prewar cars

The H.R.G. enthusiast at work. Roger Williams takes time off for an oil change during a particularly muddy trial in Wales.

which are accepted by the Vintage Sports Car Club. The postwar cars, notionally eligible for postwar historic competition, are completely uncompetitive and potentially dangerous when placed in the same field as cars with a very substantial speed advantage.

Many of the cars were originally sold overseas, or have subsequently been exported, and enthusiasts such as Tom Melahn and Gary Ford have had considerable competition successes in events promoted by the Vintage Sports Car Club of America. It is perhaps a sad commentary on the British obsession for pigeon-holing that the cars, designed by one of Britain's motoring pioneers, and with such a wonderful competition record, should now be consigned to the lock-up of history.

Appendix

13

Facts and figures

Summary of principal specifications

Statistics all too frequently confuse, rather than support, facts. However, the following tables should prove useful to the student of history, providing too many hard-and-fast conclusions are not drawn from them. The factory did keep basic records and data but these were intended for practical use, not for posterity to wax academic over.

	1½-litre	1500 W series	1500 WS series	1100	Twin-cam
Cylinders	4	4	4	4	4
Bore	69mm	68mm	73mm	60mm	73mm
Stroke	100mm	103mm	89.4mm	95mm	89.6mm
Capacity	1,496cc	1,496cc	1,497cc	1,074cc	1,497cc
Valve operation	OHV	OHC	OHC	OHC	2 OHC
Compression ratio	7.5:1	7.0:1	7.2:1	7.75:1	8.8:1
Ignition	magneto	coil/magneto	coil	coil	coil
Carburettors	2 SU	2 SU	2 SU	2 SU	2 SU/2 Solex
Tank capacity	15gal	10gal	10gal	10gal	12gal
Wheelbase	8ft 7in	8ft 7in	8ft 7in	8ft 3½in	8ft 0in
Track	4ft 0in	4ft 0in	4ft 0in	4ft 0in	4ft 0in
Length	12ft 0in	12ft 0in	12ft 0in	11ft 10½in	12ft 7in
Width	4ft 7in	4ft 7in	4ft 7in	4ft 7in	4ft 10in
Approx. weight	1,570lb	1,620lb	1,640lb	1,540lb	1,620lb

Aerodynamic: the Aerodynamic model had the same specification as the W series 1500 with the following exceptions: tank capacity 11gal, length 13ft 6in, width 4ft 10in, approximate weight 1,710lb.

Typical performance figures

By combining the results of various road tests it is possible to arrive at a representative set of figures for the performance of each model in standard trim. Many cars, of course, particularly those used in competition, were 'breathed on' in various ways to improve their performance.

	1½-litre	1500	1100
Acceleration:			
0-30mph	4.0sec	5.2sec	4.2sec
0-50mph	9.8sec	10.6sec	10.8sec
Standing ¼ mile	19.4sec	19.2sec	21.5sec
Maximum speed	92mph	86mph	78mph
Maximum power output	58bhp	61bhp	38bhp

Summary of production

Model:	1½-litre		1500			1100	others
Series:	A	W	W	W(Aero)	WS	S	
1935	1						
1936	5						
1937	10	1					
1938		8				1	1 W/T
1939		1				7	
1940-45				1			
1946			3	3		12	
1947			18	31		19	
1948			37			7	
1949			14	10		1	3*
1950			11			2	
1951			8				
1952			6				
1953			2		2		
1954					4		
1955					1		2 twin-cams
1956					5		2 twin-cams
1963							1 Ford*
1966							1 VX
Totals:	**16**	**10**	**99**	**45**	**12**	**49**	**10**

Grand total: 241 chassis

*The three special chassis built during 1949 were the Standard-powered Formula 2 single-seater, the Bristol-engined car and '1949/4', a chassis constructed to accommodate a Maserati engine. The question of whether the Bristol and Ford chassis are truly H.R.G. is a matter for discussion. There was a fifth twin-cam chassis but as this was never built up it has not been included. Neither has the special chassis for Basil Davenport's 'Spider 2'.

Prices

When the prototype car was announced the selling price was to be £375. In fact, it was slightly more: the following are indicative of prices over the years.

	1½ litre/1500	1100	Aerodynamic
1936	£395		
1938	£425	£ 289	
1946	£882	£ 812	£ 991
1947	£968	£ 812	£1,247
1948	£1,087	£1,004	
1951	£1,399		

All prices are quoted to the nearest £1 and those from 1946 onwards include purchase tax. During 1938, prices were announced for three versions which, in the event, never reached series production: further examples of the one-off Coupe would have been £475 and of the Le Mans 1½-litre, £495, while a Le Mans 1100 would have cost £365.

Colours

The factory offered four body colours in the prewar catalogues: Blue, Green, Red and Black, with black wheels in each case. Special colours could be supplied for a further £2 10s 0d.

After the war, colours were not specified in the company's catalogues, but the original range was followed, except that the wheels either matched or complemented the body and/or upholstery colour, for example, black body with matching red upholstery and wheels. Silver wheels were supplied to order with any colour.

Other body colours shown on the factory records include white, grey, metallic grey, gunmetal and maroon.

Catalogued extras

The range of extra and alternative equipment available is illustrated by the list which the factory issued in 1951.

The following is a list of Special Fittings for H.R.G. cars, which have been found of great use, and fitted to a large number of owners' cars. They are available for fitting to any H.R.G. car.

Twin spare wheel fittings, including spare wheel, tyre and tube, extra carrying shoes, double channel carrier and special strap :		
	16 x 5.50	£18 0s 0d
	17 x 4.75	£17 10s 0d

Aero screens, each including fittings	£ 2 15s 0d
Bonnet strap, including fittings	£ 3 17s 6d
Additional petrol pump, including piping, switch, etc.	£ 5 10s 0d

Andre Telecontrols, complete equipment to replace standard friction shockers, dash unit, gauge and complete with all piping connectors — £13 13s 0d

Special gear ratios for gearbox	£15 0s 0d
Scintilla Vertex 4-cylinder Magneto with suitable drive	£16 12s 6d
High compression pistons, compression ratio 8.5:1	£13 4s 0d
Extra large road racing oil sump capacity 1¾ gallons	£ 9 16s 0d
Supplementary Full-flow oil filter	£10 10s 0d
Gear lever extension up to 7in	£ 3 10s 0d
Large petrol tank	£10 0s 0d
Tropical radiator overflow tank and fittings	£ 4 0s 0d
Girling Hydraulic brakes	£47 10s 0d
Convertible Hard Top	£45 0s 0d
Fitting extra	

Notable competition results

This list of successes in competition is confined to international and major national British events. Consequently, the vast majority of achievements in trials, rallies and club racing have gone unrecorded, as have overseas national results. A full list would have included several hundred awards in the three classic MCC trials alone.

1937

Monte Carlo Rally	A.C. Scott	32nd overall and 7th in class
RAC Rally	G.H. Robins	2nd in class
Le Mans 24-hour	A.C. Scott/	
	E.A. Halford	13th overall and 2nd in class
Donington 12-hour	A.E.S. Curtis/	
	M.W. May/	
	A.C. Hess	4th overall and 3rd in class

1938

RAC Rally	G.H. Robins	3rd in class
Le Mans 24-hour	P.C.T. Clark/	
	M. Chambers	10th overall and 2nd in class

1939

RAC Rally	M.H. Lawson	1st in class
Le Mans 24-hour	P.C.T. Clark/	
	M. Chambers	14th overall and 1st in class

1946

Prescott Hill Climb	E.J. Newton	Fastest sports car and 1st in class

1947

G P des Frontieres, Chimay	P.C.T. Clark	3rd in class
Prescott Hill Climb	E.J. Newton	Twice 1st in class
Empire Trophy	P.C.T. Clark,	
	J. Scott,	Team prize
	A. Molyneux	

1948

Prescott Hill Climb	E. J. Newton	1st in class
G P des Frontieres, Chimay	J. Scott	2nd in class
	P.C.T. Clark	4th in class
Spa-Francorchamps 24-hour	J. Scott/	
	N. Gee	2nd in class
	R.B. Brock/	
	R. F. Wright	3rd in class
	P.C.T. Clark/	
	P. Marechal	4th in class. Team prize
Alpine Rally	R. Richards	Coupe des Alpes and 1st in class
	R. Richards,	
	J.Richmond,	
	J.A.H. Gott	Open Team Award

	J. Richmond,	
	J.A.H. Gott,	
	D. Mitchell	Foreign Team Award
	R. Richards,	
	J. Richmond	Special Test Awards
	R. Ross	Mt Ventoux Cup
Paris 12-hour	P.C.T. Clark/	
	P. Marechal	3rd in class
	R. Richards/	
	E. Thompson	4th in class
	H. Clapp/	
	J. Lilley,	
	J. Scott/	
	N. Gee	Winning team

1949

Le Mans 24-hour	E. Thompson/	
	J. Fairman	8th overall and 1st in class
Spa-Francorchamps 24-hour	E. Thompson/	
	J. Fairman	1st in class.
	R.B. Brock/	
	J.F. Wright	2nd in class
	J. Scott/	
	A. Pilette	3rd in class
	P.C.T. Clark/	
	M. Morris-Goodall	4th in class. Team prize, best performance by British car and British owner
Alpine Rally	J.A.H. Gott	3rd in class
	J. Richmond	4th in class
Silverstone Production Car Race	E. Thompson	1st in class
	P.C.T. Clark	2nd in class
	J. Buncombe	4th in class

1950

| Silverstone Production Car Race | G.A. Ruddock | 1st in class |
| T T Dundrod | J. Buncombe | 4th in class |

1951

Alpine Rally	J.A.H. Gott	Coupe des Alpes and 1st in class
	W. Shepherd	2nd in class
Paris-St Raphael Rally	Mrs N. Mitchell	2nd in class
Silverstone Production Car Race	G.A. Ruddock	2nd in class
	J.V.S. Brown	3rd in class
RAC Rally	J.V.S. Brown	1st in class
	Mrs N. Mitchell	2nd in class

1952

| Alpine Rally | G. Hope-Scott | 3rd in class |

1953

| RAC Rally | N.T. Lithgow | 1st in class |

Winners of the Directors' Salver

1961	Brian Symes	NPC 532		1973	Richard Clark	DKO 768
1962	Brian Symes	NPC 532		1974	Roger Newton	DCD 215/GRE 134
1963	Ted Dennis	TMX 355		1975	Roger Newton	DCD 215/GRE 134
1964	Roger Williams	HSF 256		1976	David Uglow	DRL 540
1965	Ian Dussek	LHT 670		1977	David Uglow	DRL 540
1966	Ted Dennis	TMX 355		1978	Richard Clark	DKO 768
1967	Roger Williams	HSF 256		1979	Richard Clark	DKO 768
1968	Roger Williams	HSF 256		1980	Richard Clark	DKO 768
1969	Jem Wilyman	JKR 253		1981	Richard Clark	DKO 768
1970	Roger Newton	DCD 215		1982	Richard Clark	DKO 768
1971	Rob Dennis	MPD 975		1983	Richard Clark	DKO 768
1972	Roger Newton	DCD 215/GRE 134		1984	Richard Clark	DKO 768

Specification of the 1949 Le Mans lightweights

Chassis   Standard 1500 chassis

Suspension   Front, standard 1500. Rear, semi-elliptic springs with Rotoflo dampers.

Brakes   H.R.G. mechanical with Ferodo VG95 linings. Extra air scoops in backplates for cooling.

Engine   4-cylinder, bore and stroke 68mm x 103mm, capacity 1,496cc.Compression ratio 8:1. Glacier racing bearings.

Lubrication   2-gallon ribbed alloy sump with 1-gallon reserve tank, controlled from cockpit. Tecalemit filter-cooler on front chassis crossmember.

Cooling   Gallay radiator with water pump feeding positioned jets in cylinder head.

Valves   Specially-fabricated sodium-filled pattern.

Carburettors   Twin 1$\frac{1}{4}$in SU.

Electrical System   Lucas Racing Magneto.

Sparking Plugs   Champion L11s

Gear Ratios   Close ratio 21 x 34 tooth box. First 11.45:1, second 7.16:1, third 4.63:1, Top 3.7:1.

Tyres and Wheels   Front — Dunlop Racing 4.50 x 16 Rear — Dunlop Racing 5.25 x 18

Clutch   8in diameter Borg and Beck, RYZ lining.

Rear Axle   ENV, 3.7:1 final drive ratio

Body	20swg aluminium, mounted flexibly at 8 points. Weight 50lb.	**Instruments**	5in rev counter incorporating clock. 2in oil temperature, water temperature, oil pressure and ammeter gauges.
Fuel Tank	18-gallon capacity with twin $4\frac{1}{2}$in quick-action fillers.		
Fuel System	Twin $\frac{3}{8}$in fuel lines feeding via 2 SU pumps. Zenith filter.	**Controls**	Twin pump switches, choke, starter, side and tail lamps, headlamps, dash lamp, magneto and dipswitch.
Battery	Single 12-volt, 70-amp/hour	**Screens**	Full-width wire-mesh screen and aero screen.
Silencer	Small 'Brooklands' type.		
Lights	Lucas headlamps, incorporating pilot lights. Fog lamp. Recognition light on offside. Twin tail lamps.	**Length**	12ft 6in
		Height	3ft 2in
		Width	3ft $2\frac{1}{2}$in
		Road Weight	1,365lb dry.

Bibliography

The maintenance manual issued by the company and reissued by the Association covers almost every aspect of H.R.G. ownership from a technical angle.

The following contain frequent reference to H.R.G. cars and their drivers:
Wheelspin, More Wheelspin and *Wheelspin Abroad* by C.A.N. May (Foulis).
Speed and a Microphone by Robin Richards (Kimber).
Sports Car Bodywork by B.W. Locke (Batsford).
Rallies and Trials by S.C.H. Davis (Iliffe).

Previous publications on H.R.G. history were an 18-page article in *Automobile Quarterly Vol 15 No 1* (Automobile Quarterly Inc, USA) and Profile number 58, *The "1500" & "1100" H.R.G.s, 1935-1956* (Profile Publications).

There were many road tests and similar articles including:

The Autocar
December 18, 1936	1½-litre
May 14, 1937	1½-litre
July 14, 1939	1100

May 17, 1946	Aerodynamic and 1100
January 30, 1948	Aerodynamic
December 2, 1948	1500
December 16, 1949	Le Mans lightweight
February 25, 1955	Twin-cam

Light Car
November 15, 1935	1½-litre
March 31, 1939	1100

Autosport
October 6, 1950	1500
February 11, 1955	Twin-cam

The Motor
July 4, 1939	1100
October 6, 1948	1500/1100
October 20, 1948	1500
February 25, 1955	Twin-cam

Motor Sport
June 1937	1½-litre
January 1949	1500

Speed
July 1938	1½-litre

Finally
A motorist saw his doctor about an internal disorder: 'You must give up horse riding' he was told. But the patient had never been on a horse in his life — he did, however, drive an H.R.G.